# READ & SPEAK
# KOREAN
## FOR BEGINNERS

### The Easiest Way to Learn to Communicate Right Away!

Series concept
**Jane Wightwick**

Korean edition
**Sunjeong Shin**

Illustrations by
**Leila Gaafar**

New York   Chicago   San Francisco   Lisbon   London   Madrid   Mexico City
Milan   New Delhi   San Juan   Seoul   Singapore   Sydney   Toronto

1 2 3 4 5 6 7 8 9 10 11 12 13 14 15 16 17 18 19 20 21   VLP/VLP   0 9 8

ISBN 978-0-07-154441-2 (book)
MHID      0-07-154441-0 (book)

ISBN 978-0-07-154440-5 (book & CD package)
MHID      0-07-154440-2 (book & CD package)

Library of Congress Control Number: 2007934607

McGraw-Hill books are available at special quantity discounts to use as premiums and sales promotions or for use in corporate training programs. To contact a representative, please visit the Contact Us pages at www.mhprofessional.com.

**Other titles in this series:**

*Read and Speak Arabic for Beginners*
*Read and Speak Chinese for Beginners*
*Read and Speak Greek for Beginners*
*Read and Speak Japanese for Beginners*

**Related titles:**

*Your First 100 Words in Korean*

This book is printed on acid-free paper.

✳ *plus...*

*8 tear-out cards for fun games*

*Audio CD to enhance your learning*

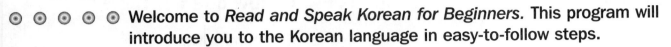

Welcome to *Read and Speak Korean for Beginners.* This program will introduce you to the Korean language in easy-to-follow steps.

The focus is on enjoyment and understanding, on reading words rather than writing them yourself. Through activities and games you'll learn how to read and speak basic Korean in less time than you thought possible.

You'll find these features in your program:

| | |
|---|---|
| **Key Words** | see them written and hear them on the CD to improve your pronunciation |
| **Language Focuses** | clear, simple explanations of language points to help you build up phrases for yourself |
| **Activities** | practice what you have learned in reading, listening, and speaking activities |
| **Games** | with tear-out components. Challenge yourself or play with a friend. A great, fun way to review |
| **Audio CD** | hear the key words and phrases and take part in interactive listening and speaking activities. You'll find the track numbers next to the activities in your book |

If you want to give yourself extra confidence with reading the script, you will find *Your First 100 Words in Korean* the ideal pre-course companion to this program. *Your First 100 Words in Korean* introduces the Korean script through 100 key everyday words, many of which also feature in *Read and Speak Korean for Beginners.*

So now you can take your first steps in Korean with confidence, enjoyment, and a real sense of progress.

*Whenever you see the audio CD symbol, you'll find listening and speaking activities on the CD included with this book. The symbol shows the track number.*

*Track 1 is an introduction to the sounds of Korean. Listen to this before you start and come back to it again at later stages if you need to.*

# Key Words

Look at the script for each key word or phrase and try to visualize it, connecting its image to the pronunciation you hear on your CD.

안녕하세요
**annyeong-haseyo**   *hello*

저는 **jeoneun**   *I*

이에요 **-ieyo**   *am/are/is*

안녕히 가세요
**annyeong-hi gaseyo**   *goodbye ("go in peace," said to someone leaving)*

안녕히 계세요
**annyeong-hi gyeseyo**   *goodbye ("stay in peace," said to someone staying)*

Korean names:

이수진
**i-sujin**   *Sujin Lee (female)*

김민준
**gim-minjun**   *Minjun Kim (male)*

최영철
**choe-yeongcheol**   *Yeongcheol Choi (male)*

박진희
**bak-jinhi**   *Jinhi Park (female)*

*The Korean "Hangeul" script is very logical – words are generally written as they sound. The Hangeul alphabet consists of consonants and vowels which combine to make syllables. The letters that make up an individual syllable are written together in a square shape. All words in Korean are composed of one or more syllables. The pronunciation is shown in the official romanization system.*

*You will find an overview of the script and the pronunciation in the reference section on page 89, but don't expect to take it all in at once. Concentrate only on some of the more recognizable syllables you meet in the Key Words for the moment and build up gradually from there. Look carefully at the script while listening to the CD, connecting the image to the pronunciation you hear.*

# How do you say it?

Join the script to the pronunciation, as in the example.

annyeong-hi gaseyo      이수진

jeoneun      안녕히 계세요

gim-minjun      저는

annyeong-haseyo      안녕하세요

ieyo      김민준

annyeong-hi gyeseyo      안녕히 가세요

i-sujin      이에요

# What does it mean?

Now say the Korean out loud and write the English next to each.

안녕하세요 _hello_      이에요 _____

김민준 _____      이수진 _____

안녕히 계세요 _____      저는 _____

**TOPIC 1: What's your name?**

# Language Focus

⊙ ⊙ ⊙ ⊙ To introduce yourself you can say 저는 ... 이에요 **jeoneun ... -ieyo** (*I am ...*) with your name in the middle.

> 저는 최영철이에요. **jeoneun choe-yeongcheol-ieyo**
> *I am Yeongcheol Choi.*
>
> 저는 마이클이에요. **jeoneun maikeul-ieyo**
> *I am Michael.*

⊙ ⊙ ⊙ ⊙ 저는 **jeoneun** is actually made up of the word for "*I*" – 저 **jeo** – followed by 는 **neun** a particle which shows that the word before is the subject of the sentence. 는 **neun** doesn't have a direct translation, but means something like "*as for.*" 이에요 **-ieyo** is a verb ending that comes after the name and here means *am*. So the Korean sentence actually reads "*I (as for) Michael am.*"

⊙ ⊙ ⊙ In Korean honorific words and verb endings exist to express politeness. They are derived from social structure. For example, people who are younger or lower in status show respect for the older or superior people. There are three tiers in verb ending usage: plain form, polite form and honorific form. You cannot use the honorific form when you talk about yourself. 이에요 **-ieyo** is a polite ending. You can also use another, more formal, polite ending 입니다 **-imnida**, for example, 저는 마이클입니다. **jeoneun maikeul-imnida** (*I am Michael*).

⊙ ⊙ When you address someone directly, you need to add a title 씨 **-ssi** (*Miss/Ms./Mr./Mrs.*) to the end of the name.

> 안녕하세요, 영철씨. **annyung-haseyo, yeongcheol-ssi**
> *Hello, YeongCheol.*

TRACK NUMBER 3

⊙
⊙ *Practice introducing yourself and learn some*
⊙ *useful replies on your CD.*
⊙

## ACTIVITIES

# What are they saying?

Write the correct number in the word balloons.

1 안녕하세요. 저는 이수진이에요.
**annyung-haseyo. jeoneun i-sujin-ieyo**

2 안녕하세요, 영철씨. **annyung-haseyo, yeongcheol-ssi**

3 안녕히 가세요. **annyeonghi gaseyo**

4 안녕하세요, 진희씨. **annyung-haseyo, jinhi-ssi**

# What do you hear?

Work out the phrases below. Then listen and check (✔) the two phrases you hear on your audio CD.

TRACK NUMBER
4

1 안녕하세요. ☐

2 안녕히 가세요, 진희씨. ☐

3 저는 이수진이에요. ☐

4 안녕하세요, 수진씨. ☐

5 안녕히 가세요, 영철씨. ☐

**TOPIC 1: What's your name?**

# Key Words

| | |
|---|---|
| 이름 **ireum** | *name* |
| 뭐? **mwo?** | *what?* |
| 이름이 뭐예요? **ireum-i mwo-yeyo?** | *what's your name?* |
| 고맙습니다 **gomap-seumnida** | *thank you* |
| 천만에요 **cheonman-eyo** | *you're welcome* |

# Language Focus

The question *What's your name?* is formed as follows: 이름 **ireum** *(name)* + 이 **-i** *(subject particle)* + 뭐 **mwo** *(what)* + 예요 **-yeyo** *(verb ending "is")*, literally "*name (as for) what is?.*" The same question would be used for "*What's his name?,*" or "*What's her name?.*" The context will make it clear.

Koreans will give their family name before the first name, for example, 저는 김영순이에요 **jeoneun gim-yeongsun-ieyo**. *I'm Yeongsun Kim.* Here 김 **gim** is the family name and 영순 **yeongsun** is the first name.

> 이름이 뭐예요? **ireumi mwo-yeyo?**
> *What's your name?*
>
> 저는 정지현이에요. **jeoneun jeong-jihyeon-ieyo.**
> *I'm Jihyeon Jeong.*

You can omit 저는 **jeoneun**: 정지현이에요. **jeong-jihyeon-ieyo** *(I) am Jihyeon Jeong*; 제인이에요. **jane-ieyo** *(I) am Jane.*

**TOPIC 1:** What's your name?

# Speaking practice

Practice the Korean you have learned so far.

# What does it mean?

Match the English word balloons to the Korean.

For example: 1b

1 You're welcome.

2 Hello.

a 저는 혜정이에요.

b 천만에요.

3 What's your name?

4 Goodbye.

c 안녕하세요.

d 고맙습니다.

5 I'm Hyejeong.

6 Thank you.

e 이름이 뭐예요?

f 안녕히 계세요.

# Which word?

Write the correct number of the word in the box to complete the conversation, as in the example.

안녕 __2__.

_____하세요.

1 이에요   2 하세요

_____최 진만이에요. 이름이_____?

3 뭐예요   4 저는   5 안녕

김수정_____.

**TOPIC 1:** What's your name?

# Language Focus

◎ ◎ ◎ ◎ ◎ Most Korean names are made up of a single-syllable family name with a double-syllable first name, although occasionally you will find double-syllable surnames, and single- or triple-syllable first names.

◎ ◎ ◎ ◎ Foreign names are phonetically represented so they may sound slightly different. This is particularly noticeable if a name ends with a consonant (except *n*, *m*, *r* or *l*). Koreans tend to pronounce the last consonant of the name separately by adding a vowel sound **eu** or **i**. For example, 제크 **jekeu** *(Jack)*, 라지 **laji** *(Raj)*

◎ ◎ ◎ Some English sounds that do not exist in Korean, such as *f*, *th*, *v*, and *z*, are pronounced as their nearest Korean equivalents (**p**, **ss**, **b** and **j**). For example, 제프 **jepeu** *(Geoff)*, 데이비드 **deibideu** *(David)*.

# What are their names?

Can you work out these common English names in Korean script?
Use the script tables on pages 89–90 to help you work them out.

| | | | |
|---|---|---|---|
| 사라 | _Sarah_ (sara)_____ | 팀 | _____ |
| 헨렌 | _____ | 켄 | _____ |
| 메리 | _____ | 마크 | _____ |
| 리사 | _____ | 로버트 | _____ |

## ACTIVITY

# In or out?

Who is in the office today and who is out at meetings? Look at the wallchart and write the names in English in the correct column, as in the example.

| | |
|---|---|
| 사라 | ✔ |
| 수진 | ✔ |
| 라지 | ✘ |
| 팀 | ✔ |
| 마이클 | ✘ |
| 헨렌 | ✘ |
| 민준 | ✔ |
| 영철 | ✔ |
| 로버트 | ✘ |
| 진희 | ✘ |

| IN | OUT |
|---|---|
| *Sarah* | |

**TOPIC 1:** What's your name?

# The Name Game

1. Tear out Game Card 1 at the back of your book and cut out the name cards (leave the sentence-build cards at the bottom of the sheet for the moment).

2. Put the cards Korean side up and see if you can recognize the names. Turn over the cards to see if you were correct.

3. Keep shuffling the cards and testing yourself until you can read all the names.

4. Then cut out the extra sentence-build cards at the bottom of the sheet and make mini-dialogs. For example:

– annyeong-haseyo. ireumi mwo-yeyo?

– jeoneun tim-ieyo.

5. You can also play with a friend. Make mini-dialogs for each other to read. If you both have a book, you can play pairs (pelmanism) with both sets of cards, saying the words as you turn over the cards.

# Key Words

Some names of countries end with the syllable 국 **guk** meaning "country" (although the word by itself actually means "soup"!) Other countries and cities are written phonetically in most cases.

To learn new words, try covering the English and looking at the Korean script and pronunciation. Start from the first word and work your way to the last word seeing if you can remember the English. Then do the same but this time starting from the bottom and moving up to the first word. See if you can go down and up three times without making any mistakes. Then try looking only at the Korean characters and see if you can remember the pronunciation and meaning. When you can recognize all the words, cover the Korean and this time look at the English, saying the Korean out loud.

**TOPIC 2: Where are you from?**

# Where are the countries?

Write the number next to the country, as in the example.

캐나다 <u>1</u>　　　아일랜드__　　　영국__　　　중국 __

일본 __　　　　　한국__　　　　호주 __　　　　미국 __

# How do you say it?

Join the English to the pronunciation and the Korean script, as in the example.

| England | ail-landeu | 한국 |
| Korea | hoju | 중국 |
| Ireland | miguk | 호주 |
| city | yeong-guk | 도시 |
| China | nara | 아일랜드 |
| Canada | dosi | 캐나다 |
| America | han-guk | 영국 |
| country | jung-guk | 일본 |
| Australia | ilbon | 미국 |
| Japan | cae-nada | 나라 |

# Which city?

See if you can figure out the cities using the English in the box to help you.

| Seoul | New York | Washington | Los Angeles |
| Busan | Sydney | London | |

런던 _____London_____

서울 _____

부산 _____

로스 엔젤레스 _____

시드니 _____

뉴욕 _____

워싱턴 _____

**TOPIC 2:** Where are you from?

# Language Focus

To form a nationality, Korean adds 사람 **saram**, meaning *person* or *people*, to the name of the country. So 한국사람 **hanguk-saram** means *Korean (person/people)*, 영국사람 **yeongguk-saram** means *English (person/people)*, etc. To form sentences, use the verb ending 이에요 **-ieyo** that you learned in Topic 1.

> 저는 중국사람이에요. **jeoneun jungguk-saram-ieyo**
> *I'm Chinese.*
>
> 저는 미국사람이에요. **jeoneun miguk-saram-ieyo**
> *I'm American.*

To say where you come from use the expression 저는 ...에서 왔어요 **jeoneun ...eseo wasseoyo** *(I'm from...)*. 에서 **eseo** is an ending with a meaning similar to the English preposition *from*, and 왔어요 **wasseoyo** means *came*. By adding the name of a city or a country before **eseo** you can say where you are from. If you want to mention both the country and the city you are from, you simply say the name of the city directly after the country.

> 저는 한국에서 왔어요. **jeoneun hanguk-eseo wasseoyo**
> *I come from Korea.*
>
> 저는 뉴욕에서 왔어요. **jeoneun nyu-yok-eseo wasseoyo**
> *I come from New York.*
>
> 저는 호주 시드니에서 왔어요 **jeoneun hoju sideuni-eseo wasseoyo** *I come from Sydney (in) Australia.*

To ask where someone is from, use the question word 어디? **eodi** *(where?)* together with 에서 왔어요 **eseo wasseoyo**:

> 어디에서 왔어요? **eodi-eseo wasseoyo?**
> *Where do you come from?*

TRACK NUMBER
8

> Listen to six different people introducing themselves and see
> if you can understand where they are from.

**ACTIVITIES**

# Where are they from?

Join the people to their nationalities, as in the example. Listen again to track 8 on your CD and look back at the names and countries if you need to remind yourself.

박진화　　　　미국
마이클　　　　영국
교코　　　　　캐나다
제인　　　　　중국
왕밍　　　　　한국
켄　　　　　　일본

# Where are *you* from?

TRACK NUMBER **9**

Now say where you're from.
Follow the prompts on your audio CD.

# Key Words

TRACK NUMBER **10**

| | | |
|---|---|---|
| 사람 **saram** | person/people | 어디에서 왔어요? *Where do you*<br>**eodi-eseo wasseoyo** *come from?* |
| 에서 **eseo** | from | |
| 어디 **eodi** | where? | 저는...에서 왔어요 *I come from ...*<br>**jeoneun ...-eseo**<br>**wasseoyo** |

**TOPIC 2:** Where are you from?

# Language Focus

⊙ ⊙ ⊙ ⊙ ⊙ English often refers to other people as *he* or *she*: *He is American*, *She is from New York*, etc. Korean speakers rarely use *he* or *she*. Instead they prefer to use the person's name followed by the title 씨 **-ssi** *(Miss/Ms./Mr./Mrs.)*.

> 수진씨는 한국에서 왔어요.
> **sujinssi-neun hanguk-eseo wasseoyo**
> *Sujin comes from Korea.*
>
> 제인씨는 영국사람이에요.
> **jeinssi-neun yeongguk-saram-ieyo**
> *Jane is English.*

⊙ ⊙ ⊙ ⊙ Generally, you can omit pronouns such as *I*, *you*, *he* or *she* altogether in Korean if the context is clear.

> 캐나다에서 왔어요.
> **caenada-eseo wasseoyo**
> *(I) come from Canada.*
>
> 어디에서 왔어요?
> **eodi-eseo wasseoyo?**
> *Where do (you) come from?*
>
> 중국사람이에요?
> **jungguk-saram-ieyo?**
> *Are (you) Chinese?*

⊙ ⊙ ⊙ Notice from the last example that you can turn a statement into a question in Korean by simply using a questioning tone at the end.

**TOPIC 2: Where are you from?**

# Who's from where?

Make questions and answers about where these people come from, as in the example.

**1**

피터 piteo

피터씨는 어디에서 왔어요?
**piteossi-neun eodi-eseo wasseoyo?**
*Where does Peter come from?*

피터씨는 미국 뉴욕에서 왔어요.
**piteossi-neun miguk nyuyok-eseo wasseoyo** *Peter comes from New York (in) America.*

**2**

교코 kyoko

**3**

헨렌 helen

**4**

마크 makeu

**5**

메리 meri

**6**

수진 sujin

**7**

왕밍 wangming

**8**

팀 tim

**TOPIC 2: Where are you from?**

# Listen and check

Listen to the conversation on your audio CD and decide if these sentences are true or false.

|  |  | True | False |
|---|---|---|---|
| 1 | The woman's name is Sophie. | ☐ | ☐ |
| 2 | She comes from Canada. | ☐ | ☐ |
| 3 | The man's name is Yeongcheol. | ☐ | ☐ |
| 4 | He comes from Seoul. | ☐ | ☐ |
| 5 | They are already friends. | ☐ | ☐ |

# What does it mean?

Now read the Korean you heard in the conversation and match it with the English, as in the example.

*I'm Lucy.*                 저는 캐나다사람이에요.

*Pleased to meet you.*     한국 부산에서 왔어요.

*Hello.*               저는루 시예요.

*I'm Canadian.*        이름이 뭐예요?

*What's your name?*     안녕하세요.

*I come from Busan in Korea.*    만나서 반갑습니다.

# What does it mean?

Try to work out each of these sentences. It will help if you break them up into the separate words and phrases. Look back at the Key Word panels if you need help.

Then read the sentences out loud when you have figured them out and write the English next to each, as in the example.

**1** 저는 루시예요.          <u>I'm Lucy.</u>

**2** 저는 캐나다사람이에요.          _____

**3** 수진씨는 한국사람이에요.          _____

**4** 이름이 뭐예요?          _____

**5** 저는 박진희예요.          _____

**6** 팀씨는 어디에서 왔어요?          _____

**7** 팀씨는 영국에서 왔어요.          _____

**8** 헬렌씨는 미국에서 왔어요.          _____

You can compare your pronunciation of the sentences with the models on your audio CD.

Now complete this description of yourself. Read the sentences out loud, adding your own name and where you come from.

저는 ...이에요.

저는 ... ...에서 왔어요.

**TOPIC 2:** Where are you from?

# The Flag Game

1. Tear out Game Card 2.

2. Find a die and counter(s).

3. Put the counter(s) on START.

4. Throw the die and move that number of squares.

5. When you land on a flag, you must ask and answer the appropriate question for that country. For example:

어디에서 왔어요?
**eodi-eseo wasseoyo?**
*Where do you come from?*

캐나다에서 왔어요.
**caenada-eseo wasseoyo**
*I come from Canada.*

6. If you can't remember the question or answer, you must go back to the square you came from. You must throw the exact number to finish.

7. You can challenge yourself or play with a friend.

**TOPIC 2:** Where are you from?

# Key Words

| 의자 **uija** | chair | 문 **mun** | door |
| 탁자 **takja** | table | 창문 **changmun** | window |
| 텔레비전 **telle-bijeon** | television | 펜 **pen** | pen |
| 책 **chaek** | book | 잡지 **japji** | magazine |
| 가방 **gabang** | bag | 소파 **sopa** | sofa |
| 컴퓨터 **keompyuteo** | computer | 전화 **jeonhwa** | telephone |

⊚ *Many words in modern Korean have been borrowed from English,*
⊚ *for example "computer," "pen," and "sofa."*
⊚ *The pronunciation of these loan words has sometimes been*
⊚ *slightly adapted to Korean speech patterns, but you can just say*
⊚ *the word as you would in English and be perfectly understood.*

**TOPIC 3:** What's this?

# Language Focus

◎ ◎ ◎ ◎ Korean nouns do not have articles (a/an, the). Plurals are also
simple. You can usually use the same word as the singular.
So 책 **chaek** can mean *book, a book, the book, books,* or *the books.*

# What does it mean?

Match the Korean with the pictures, then write the pronunciation and the English.

가방 _____

컴퓨터 _____

문 _____

창문 *changmun* window(s)

전화 _____

펜 _____

의자 _____

탁자 _____

소파 _____

텔레비전 _____

책 _____

잡지 _____

**TOPIC 3:** What's this?

# Word Square

Can you find the eight household words in the word square? Circle them and write the English, as in the example. The words can be horizontal or vertical.

| 리 | 에 | 파 | 소 | 젤 | 레 | 스 | 컴 |
|---|---|---|---|---|---|---|---|
| 엔 | 로 | 스 | 파 | 턴 | 싱 | 잡 | 지 |
| 욕 | 뉴 | 로 | 턴 | 버 | 다 | 캐 | 나 |
| 퓨 | 전 | 화 | 사 | 다 | 라 | 인 | 예 |
| 가 | 국 | 인 | 영 | 컴 | 퓨 | 터 | 인 |
| 방 | 마 | 자 | 의 | 스 | 버 | 캐 | 탁 |
| 전 | 헨 | 크 | 턴 | 버 | 다 | 의 | 자 |
| 텔 | 레 | 비 | 전 | 지 | 예 | 수 | 요 |

_computer_ _____

_____

_____

_____

_____

_____

_____

# Odd One Out

Which is the odd one out? Circle the word in each row that doesn't belong.

탁자 * 의자 * 소파 * 이름

한국 * 전화 * 호주 * 일본

사람 * 책 * 텔레비전 * 잡지

창문 * 수진 * 진희 * 사라

고맙습니다 * 천만에요 * 컴퓨터 * 안녕하세요

**TOPIC 3: What's this?**

# Language Focus

⊙ ⊙ ⊙ ⊙ You have already met the question 뭐예요? **mwo-yeyo?** (뭐 **mwo** *what* + 예요 **yeyo** *is*) in the expression 이름이 뭐예요? **ireumi mwoyeyo?** *what's your name?* **To ask** *what's this?* insert 이것이 **igeosi** *this (as for)* in place of the word 이름이 **ireum-i.**

> 이것이 뭐예요? **igeosi mwoyeyo?** *What's this?*

⊙ ⊙ ⊙ ⊙ To answer, use the following:

이것은 **igeoseun** *this (as for)* + object + 이에요 **-ieyo** <u>or</u> 예요 **-yeyo**

If the word for the object ends with a consonant, for example 펜 **pen**, add 이에요 **-ieyo**. If it ends with a vowel, for example 소파 **sopa**, use 예요 **-yeyo**.

> 이것은 의자예요. **igeoseun uija-yeyo**
> *This is a chair./These are chairs.*
>
> 이것은 가방이에요. **igeoseun gabang-ieyo**
> *This is a bag./These are bags.*

⊙ ⊙ ⊙ To ask a question such as *Is this a chair?* just raise the intonation at the end of the sentence. Watch out for the Korean word 네 **ne** which means *"yes."* *"No"* is 아니오 **anio**. 이것이 **igeosi** can be shortened to 이게 **ige** in a question and 이것은 **igeoseun** is also often shortened to 이건 **igeon** or dropped altogether in the answer.

> 이게 문이에요? **ige mun-ieyo?** *Is this a door?*
> 네, 이건 문이에요. **ne, igeon mun-ieyo** *Yes, it's a door.*
> 아니오, 창문이에요. **anio, changmun-ieyo**
> *No, it's a window.*

**ACTIVITIES**

# Your turn to speak

Now ask what things are.
Follow the prompts on your audio CD.

# What is it?

Look at the pictures of everyday objects from unusual angles. Then read the sentences and decide which picture they describe, as in the example.

**1** 이것은 의자예요. _e_    **4** 이것은 전화예요. __    **7** 이건 펜이에요. __

**2** 이것은 컴퓨터예요. __    **5** 이건 문이에요. __    **8** 이건 가방이에요. __

**3** 이것은 소파예요. __    **6** 이건 텔레비전이에요. __

**TOPIC 3:** What's this?

# Key Words

TRACK NUMBER 15

녹차 **nokcha**      *green tea*

커피 **keopi**      *coffee*

샌드위치 **saendeuwichi**   *sandwich*

케이크 **keikeu**      *cake*

떡볶이 **tteokbokki**      *rice cake in spicy sauce*

튀김 **twigim**      *deep-fried vegetables*

# Language Focus

⊙ ⊙ ⊙ ⊙ ⊙ **To say** *I'd like …* **use** 주세요 **juseyo** (literally *"give"*) **after the object you want.**

> 커피 주세요. **keopi juseyo** *I'd like a coffee.*
> 녹차 주세요. **nokcha juseyo** *I'd like green tea.*

⊙ ⊙ ⊙ ⊙ **To ask for more than one item, link them using** 과 **gwa** **if the word before ends with a consonant, or** 와 **wa** **if it ends with a vowel.**

> 튀김과 케이크 주세요. **twigim-gwa keikeu juseyo**
> *I'd like twigim and a cake.*
>
> 커피와 녹차 주세요. **keopi-wa nokcha juseyo**
> *I'd like a coffee and a green tea.*

⊙ ⊙ ⊙ **The Korean equivalent of** *Here you are* **is** 여기 있어요 **yeogi isseoyo** (**yeogi** = *here*; **isseoyo** = *is/have*).

> 떡볶이 주세요. **tteokbokki juseyo** *I'd like tteokbokki.*
> 여기 있어요. **yeogi isseoyo** *Here you are/Here it is.*
> 고맙습니다. **gomap-seumnida** *Thank you.*
> 천만에요. **cheonmaneyo** *You're welcome.*

**TOPIC 3:** What's this?

# Who orders what?

What are the cus͏͏ rs ordering? Listen to your
CD and check wh͏a͏ ey order, as in the example.

TRACK NUMBER
16

|  | green tea | coffee | sandwich | cake | twigim (vegetables) | tteokbokki (rice cakes) |
|---|---|---|---|---|---|---|
| Customer 1 | ✓ |  |  |  |  | ✓ |
| Customer 2 |  |  |  |  |  |  |
| Customer 3 |  |  |  |  |  |  |
| Customer 4 |  |  |  |  |  |  |
| Customer 5 |  |  |  |  |  |  |

Now look at the table above and pretend you are ordering for yourself. For example:

녹차와 떡볶이 주세요. **nokcha-wa tteokbokki juseyo**

**TOPIC 3:** What's this?

# Unscramble the conversation

Can you put this conversation in the correct order?

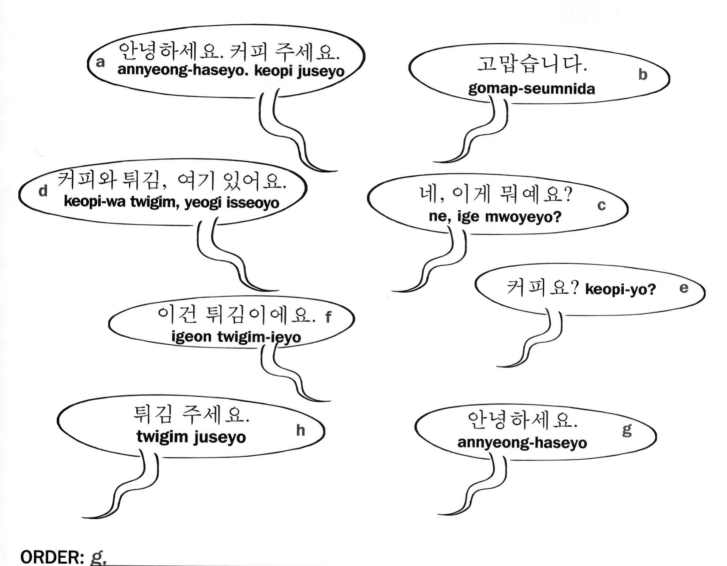

a 안녕하세요. 커피 주세요.
annyeong-haseyo. keopi juseyo

b 고맙습니다.
gomap-seumnida

d 커피와 튀김, 여기 있어요.
keopi-wa twigim, yeogi isseoyo

c 네, 이게 뭐예요?
ne, ige mwoyeyo?

e 커피요? keopi-yo?

f 이건 튀김이에요.
igeon twigim-ieyo

h 튀김 주세요.
twigim juseyo

g 안녕하세요.
annyeong-haseyo

ORDER: g,_____

Now check your answer with the conversation on your audio CD.

TRACK NUMBER
17

# At the café

TRACK NUMBER
18

Your turn to order now. Look at the menu below and
then you'll be ready to order from the waiter on your CD.

녹차

커피

샌드위치

케이크

떡볶이

튀김

**TOPIC 3: What's this?**

# The Café Game

1. Cut out the picture cards from Game Card 3.

2. Put the cards into a bag.

3. Shake the bag.

4. Pull out a card without looking.

5. Ask for the item on the card. For example:
녹차 주세요. **nokcha juseyo**
*I'd like a green tea.*

6. If you can ask the question out loud quickly and fluently, then put the card aside. If not, then put it back into the bag.

7. See how long it takes you to get all of the cards out of the bag. You can also play with a friend and see who can collect the most cards.

**TOPIC 3:** What's this?

# Key Words

TRACK NUMBER
19

| 방 **bang** | room | 집 **jip** | house |
| 냉장고 **naeng-jang-go** | refrigerator | 나무 **namu** | tree |
| 커튼 **keoteun** | curtains | 차 **cha** | car |
| 가스레인지 **gaseu-reinji** | cooker/hob | 개 **gae** | dog |
| 침대 **chimdae** | bed | 쥐 **jwi** | mouse |
| 그림 **geurim** | picture | 고양이 **goyangi** | cat |

# Language Focus

⊙ ⊙ ⊙ ⊙ ⊙  Korean words can be a single syllable, such as 개 **gae** (*dog*) or 집 **jip** (*house*). But more often they are a combination of two or more syllables. For example, 침대 **chimdae** (*bed*) consists of two syllables and 냉장고 **naeng-jang-go** (*refrigerator*) of three syllables.

⊙ ⊙ ⊙ ⊙  The individual letters that make up a syllable are written together in a square shape. Look at page 90 for more details on how the individual letters are combined to form syllables.

⊙ ⊙ ⊙  Notice that 차 **cha** can either mean *car* or *tea* (as in 녹차 **nokcha** *green tea*).

**TOPIC 4:** Where is it?

# What does it mean?

Join the Korean to the pronunciation and write down the meaning in English.

| | | |
|---|---|---|
| 커튼 | jwi | _____ |
| 차 | chimdae | _____ |
| 개 | geurim | _____ |
| 침대 | jip | _____ |
| 쥐 | keoteun | *curtains* |
| 그림 | gaseu-reinji | _____ |
| 집 | namu | _____ |
| 방 | naeng-jang-go | _____ |
| 냉장고 | bang | _____ |
| 나무 | cha | _____ |
| 가스레인지 | gae | _____ |

# What can you see?

Look at the picture and check (✔) the things you can see, as in the example.

| | |
|---|---|
| 침대 ✔ | 가방 ☐ |
| 의자 ☐ | 개 ☐ |
| 나무 ☐ | 냉장고 ☐ |
| 그림 ☐ | 고양이 ☐ |
| 탁자 ☐ | 방 ☐ |
| 소파 ☐ | 컴퓨터 ☐ |
| 커튼 ☐ | 펜 ☐ |
| 잡지 ☐ | 가스레인지 ☐ |
| 차 ☐ | 책 ☐ |

**TOPIC 4:** Where is it?

On Or Under?

# Key Words

안 **an** — in(side)

위 **wi** — on (top of)/ above

밑 **mit** — under

앞 **ap** — in front of

뒤 **dwi** — behind

옆 **yeop** — next to

# Language Focus

To say where something is in English we simply place the preposition (positional word) in the middle of the two objects: *The pen is <u>on</u> the table*. In Korean the preposition comes <u>after</u> the two objects and the order is *"pen (as for) table <u>on</u> is."* Notice as well that you need to use a small particle, 에 **-e**, after the preposition (*on, in,* etc.) to show that you are talking about a place.

펜은 의자 위에 있어요. **pen-eun uija wi-e isseoyo**
*The pen is on the table.*

차는 집 앞에 있어요. **cha-neun jip ap-e isseoyo**
*The car is in front of the house.*

개는 침대 밑에 있어요. **gae-neun chimdae mit-e isseoyo**
*The dog is under the bed.*

*Practice saying where things are on your CD.*

**TOPIC 4: Where is it?**

# Which word?

Put a circle around the alternative
that correctly describes each
picture, as in the example.

1 차는 집 (앞에) 있어요.
뒤에

2 텔레비전은 창문 위에 있어요.
밑에

3 그림은 소파 앞에 있어요.
위에

4 컴퓨터는 탁자 위에 있어요.
옆에

5 냉장고는 가스레인지 옆에 있어요.
위에

6 개는 의자 뒤에 있어요.
밑에

7 개는 차 안에 있어요.
위에

# Language Focus

You have met a number of "subject particles" so far. These particles are placed directly after the subject of a sentence or question and roughly translate as *"as for."* They show what it is you are talking about. There are four subject particles – two used for words ending in vowels and two for words ending in consonants.

| | subject particle | example |
|---|---|---|
| ends with vowel (e.g. 차 **cha** *car*) | 가 **-ga** | 차가 **cha-ga** |
| | 는 **-neun** | 차는 **cha-neun** |
| ends with consonant (e.g. 방 **bang** *room*) | 이 **-i** | 방이 **bang-i** |
| | 은 **-eun** | 방은 **bang-eun** |

가 **-ga** and 이 **-i** are "neutral" subject particles whereas 는 **-neun** and 은 **-eun** are "emphatic." In the sentence 펜은 탁자 위에 있어요 **pen-eun takja wie isseoyo** *The pen is on the table*, 은 **-eun** emphasises the subject 펜 **pen**. If we change 은 **-eun** to the neutral 이 **-i**, *pen* is no longer emphasized and the meaning is closer to the English *There is a* pen on the table. Here are some examples. (Remember that to form questions simply raise the intonation at the end.)

차는 집 앞에 있어요. **cha-neun jip ape isseoyo**
*The car is in front of the house.*
차가 집 앞에 있어요. **cha-ga jip ape isseoyo**
*There is a car in front of the house.*

책은 침대 위에 있어요? **chaek-eun chimdae wie isseoyo**
*Is the book on (top of) the bed?*
책이 침대 위에 있어요? **chaek-i chimdae wie isseoyo**
*Is there a book on (top of) the bed?*

◎ *Look around the room you are in at the moment, or think of a*
◎ *room you know well. Can you describe where some of the things*
◎ *are, using the Korean sentences you have learned?*

**TOPIC 4:** Where is it?

# Where are the mice?

See how many mice you can find in the picture and make sentences about them as in the example.

Example:
쥐가 가스레인지 앞에 있어요.
**jwi-ga gaseu-reinji ap-e isseoyo**
*There's a mouse in front of the stove.*

# Language Focus

Generally, placing 안 **an** *(not)* before a verb will make it negative.

저는 한국에서 왔어요.
**jeoneun hanguk-eseo wasseoyo**
*I come from Korea.* *("I-as for Korea-from came")*

저는 한국에서 안 왔어요.
**jeoneun hanguk-eseo an wasseoyo**
*I don't come from Korea.* *("I-as for Korea-from not came")*

안 **an** combines with 이에요 **-ieyo** or 예요 **-yeyo** *(am/are/is)* to produce 아니에요 **anieyo.**

저는 미국사람이에요. **jeoneun miguk-saram-ieyo**
*I'm American.*

저는 미국사람 아니에요. **jeoneun miguk-saram anieyo**
*I'm not American.*

이것은/이건 소파예요. **igeoseun/igeon sopa-yeyo**
*This is a sofa.*

이것은/이건 소파 아니에요. **igeoseun/igeon sopa anieyo**
*This isn't a sofa.*

있어요 **isseoyo** *(there is/are ... )* has its own negative: 없어요 **eopsseoyo.**

차가 집 앞에 있어요. **chaga jip ape isseoyo**
*There is a car in front of the house.*

차가 집 앞에 없어요. **chaga jip ape eopsseoyo**
*There isn't a car in front of the house.*

**TOPIC 4: Where is it?**

# No, it isn't!

Practice disagreeing! Go to your audio CD and contradict all the statements you hear.

TRACK NUMBER
22

# True or False?

Decide if the sentences describing the picture are true or false, as in the example.

| | True | False |
|---|---|---|
| 냉장고가 방 안에 있어요. | ✔ | ☐ |
| 침대가 방 안에 있어요. | ☐ | ☐ |
| 전화는 탁자 위에 있어요. | ☐ | ☐ |
| 찬장이 없어요. | ☐ | ☐ |
| 창문이 있어요. | ☐ | ☐ |
| 쥐가 탁자 밑에 없어요. | ☐ | ☐ |
| 나무가 집 뒤에 있어요. | ☐ | ☐ |
| 가스 레인지는 냉장고 옆에 있어요. | ☐ | ☐ |
| 개가 탁자 밑에 있어요. | ☐ | ☐ |
| 텔레비전이 방에 없어요. | ☐ | ☐ |

# Language Review

You're half way through *Read and Speak Korean for Beginners* – congratulations! This is a good time to summarize the main language points covered so far.

**1** There is no clear distinction between plural and singular in Korean. 사람 **saram** means both *a person* and *people*.

**2** It is important to include the subject particles: 가 **-ga** or 는 **-neun** for words ending with a vowel, and 이 **-i** or 은 **-eun** for those ending with a consonant. 은 **-eun** and 는 **-neun** are used to emphasize the subject.

**3** The equivalent in Korean of *am/is/are* is the ending 예요 **-yeyo** (for words ending in a vowel) or 이에요 **-ieyo** (for words ending in a consonant). The opposite of both is 아니에요 **anieyo**. The equivalent of *there is/are* is 있어요 **isseoyo**. The opposite is 없어요 **eopsseoyo**.

> 저는 호주사람이에요. **jeoneun hoju-saram-ieyo**
> *I'm Australian.*
>
> 저는 호주사람 아니에요. **jeoneun hoju-saram anieyo**
> *I'm not Australian.*
>
> 쥐가 침대 밑에 있어요. **jwi-ga chimdae mit-e isseoyo**
> *There's a mouse under the bed.*
>
> 쥐가 침대 밑에 없어요. **jwi-ga chimdae mit-e eopsseoyo**
> *There isn't a mouse under the bed.*

**4** In general you should use people's names rather than pronouns such as "he" or "she." You don't generally need to use the pronoun "you" at all.

**5** To ask questions, you simply raise the intonation at the end.

> 왕밍씨는 중국사람이에요. **wangmingssi-neun gungguk-saram-ieyo.** *WangMing is Chinese.*
>
> 영국 사람이에요? **yeong-guk-saram-ieyo?** *Are (you) English?*

**6** To request something, you can use the phrase 주세요 **juseyo** after the item(s) you want:
커피와 샌드위치 주세요. **keopi-wa saendeuwichi juseyo** *I'd like a coffee and a sandwich.*

**TOPIC 4: Where is it?**

# My room

(1) Tear out Game Card 4 at the back of your book and cut out the small pictures of items around the house (leave the sentence-build cards at the bottom of the sheet for the moment).

(2) Stick the pictures wherever you like on the scene below.

(3) Cut out the sentence-build cards from Game Card 4. Make and say aloud as many sentences as you can describing your room. For example:

| 그림 | 이 | 침대 | 위에 | 있어요 |

**geurim-i chimdae wi-e isseoyo**
*There's a picture above the bed.*

# Key Words

| | | | | |
|---|---|---|---|---|
| 큰 **keun** | big | 비싼 **bissan** | expensive | |
| 작은 **jageun** | small | 싼 **ssan** | inexpensive | |
| 새 **sae** | new | 아주 **aju** | very | |
| 낡은 **nalgeun** | old/worn out | 너무 **neomu** | too | |

TRACK NUMBER 23

# Language Focus

⊙ ⊙ ⊙ ⊙ ⊙ As in English, Korean adjectives (descriptive words) come before the noun they describe.

> 큰 가방 **keun gabang** *big bag/big bags*
> 새 차 **sae cha** *new car/new cars*

⊙ ⊙ ⊙ ⊙ 아주 **aju** *(very)* is placed in front of the adjective, just like in English:

> 아주 싼 커피 **aju ssan keopi** *very inexpensive coffee*

⊙ ⊙ ⊙ Note that if an adjective is not used directly before the thing it describes, it needs a verb ending, usually 요 **-yo**. Adding **-yo** can affect the pronunciation. For example, 작은 **jageun** *(small)* changes to 작아요 **jagayo** *(to be small)*, 비싼 **bissan** *(expensive)* to 비싸요 **bissayo** *(to be expensive)*.

> 그건 비싸요. **geugeon bissayo** *That's expensive.*
> 그건 너무 작아요. **geugeon neomu jagayo**
> *That's too small.*

**TOPIC 5:** What's it like?

# Can you remember?

Cover the Key Words panel on page 44. Then see if you can write out the pronunciation and meaning of the words below, as in the example.

비싼          b i s s a n                    _expensive_

큰            k _ _ _                      _____

낡은          n _ _ _ e _ _                _____

싼            _ s _ _                      _____

새            _ _ e                        _____

너무          n _ _ _ u                    _____

아주          a _ _                        _____

작은          _ _ g _ _ _                  _____

# What does it mean?

Match the Korean with the pictures. Then read the Korean out loud and write the English next to each, as in the example.

새 소파 _____

작은 커피 _____

작은 개 *(a) small dog* _____

낡은 차 _____

큰 나무 _____

작은 쥐 _____

큰 샌드위치 _____

비싼 그림 _____

# Listen and check

TRACK NUMBER
24

Listen to the conversation at the car rental company and decide if these sentences are true or false.

A useful phrase you'll hear in the dialog is: 어때요? **eottaeyo?** *How is it?*. This is often used with the meaning of *How about...?*: 골프 어때요? *How about the Golf?* ("The Golf, how is it?")

|  |  | True | False |
|---|---|---|---|
| 1 | She thinks the Golf is too expensive. | ☐ | ☐ |
| 2 | She thinks the second car offered is too big. | ☐ | ☐ |
| 3 | She likes the Fiat. | ☐ | ☐ |
| 4 | The woman's name is Susie. | ☐ | ☐ |
| 5 | She's Canadian. | ☐ | ☐ |

# Unscramble the sentences

Look at the scrambled phrases from the conversation and write the correct order in the boxes. For example, *"How about the Golf"*:

b 어때요?     a 골프

1

☐ 사람     ☐ 이에요?     ☐ 미국

2
☐ 차     ☐ 주세요     ☐ 그

3

☐ 저는     ☐ 예요     ☐ 메리

4

☐ 작아요     ☐ 그건     ☐ 너무

# Language Focus

⊙ ⊙ ⊙ ⊙ ⊙ You have already met the word 있어요 **isseoyo** with the meaning of *there is* or *there are*. You can also use this phrase to describe what you or other people have.

> 저는 낡은 탁자가 있어요. **jeoneun nalgeun takja-ga isseoyo** *I have an old table.*
>
> 수진씨는 새 컴퓨터가 있어요. **sujinssi-neun sae keompyuteo-ga isseoyo** *Sujin has a new computer.*
>
> 마이클씨는 비싼 차가 있어요. **maikeulssi-neun bissan chaga isseoyo** *Michael has an expensive car.*

⊙ ⊙ ⊙ ⊙ Remember that to ask a question, just raise the intonation at the end.

> 싼 차가 있어요? **ssan chaga isseoyo?**
> *Do you have an inexpensive car?*
>
> 선영씨는 큰 집이 있어요? **seonyeongssi-neun keun jibi isseoyo?** *Does Seonyeong have a big house?*

⊙ ⊙ ⊙ To give a short reply ("yes, I do," etc.) you need to repeat 있어요 **isseoyo**.

> 새 차가 있어요? **sae chaga isseoyo**
> *Do you have a new car?*
>
> 네, 있어요. **ne, isseoyo**
> *Yes, (I) do.*

TRACK NUMBER 25

*Now you can take part in a conversation with the car rental company. Follow the prompts on your audio CD.*

⊙ ⊙ ⊙ ⊙ ⊙ ⊙ ⊙ ⊙ ⊙ ⊙ ⊙ ⊙ ⊙ ⊙ ⊙ ⊙ ⊙ ⊙ ⊙ ⊙ ⊙ ⊙ ⊙ ⊙ ⊙ ⊙

**TOPIC 5:** What's it like?

1024680

24689111315171924681011121314151617181920

3234567891011121314151617181920

256102467891011121314151617181920

246789101114161820

# Key Words

TRACK NUMBER 26

| 머리 **meori** | head/hair (on head) | 코 **ko** | nose |
| 다리 **dari** | legs | 입 **ip** | mouth |
| 팔 **pal** | arms | 귀 **gui** | ears |
| 손가락 **son-garak** | fingers | 배 **bae** | stomach |
| 눈 **nun** | eyes | 꼬리 **kkori** | tail |

*By now you're probably feeling more confident about reading and speaking Korean. Maybe you'd like to try writing the letters and characters for yourself. Although it's fun to copy the simpler shapes, you will need to get a guide to writing Korean in order to form the words correctly. The strokes should be completed in a certain order and will need practice to perfect.*

**TOPIC 5: What's it like?**

**ACTIVITIES**

# Which word?

Circle the correct word to match the translation,
as in the example.

| | | | | | |
|---|---|---|---|---|---|
| 1 | *head/hair* | 비싼 | (머리) | 커피 | 가방 |
| 2 | *legs* | 녹차 | 커튼 | 나무 | 다리 |
| 3 | *stomach* | 배 | 저 | 씨 | 펜 |
| 4 | *mouth* | 한 | 책 | 입 | 큰 |
| 5 | *fingers* | 냉장고 | 침대 | 작은 | 손가락 |
| 6 | *tail* | 는 | 새 | 집 | 꼬리 |
| 7 | *ears* | 문 | 귀 | 뭐 | 이 |
| 8 | *nose* | 코 | 최 | 국 | 개 |
| 9 | *eyes* | 긴 | 팀 | 박 | 눈 |
| 10 | *arms* | 방 | 차 | 팔 | 김 |

**TOPIC 5:** What's it like?

# At the circus

Can you use the words in the box to complete the description of the clowns, Cheolsu and Sunhi, as in the example?

**1** 배

**2** 커요

**3** 고양이

**4** 입

**5** 작아요

**6** 낡은

철수는 눈이 ___5___ . _____ 가 커요.
그리고 손에 _____ 가방이 있어요.

순희는 코가 _____ . _____ 이 작아요.
그리고 작은 _____ 가 있어요.

# What does it look like?

What does the alien look like? Make as many sentences as you can describing the features this creature has.

We've included some more adjectives you could use to describe the alien.

**Example**

아주 큰 코가 있어요. **aju keun koga isseoyo**

*(It) has a very big nose.*

| | | |
|---|---|---|
| *beautiful* | 아름다운 | **areumdaun** |
| *ugly* | 못생긴 | **motsaenggin** |
| *fat* | 뚱뚱한 | **ttungttunghan** |
| *thin* | 마른 | **mareun** |
| *long* | 긴 | **gin** |
| *short* | 짧은 | **jjalbeun** |

# What do you have?

1. Cut out the picture cards from Game Card 5 and put them in a bag.

2. Cut out the adjective cards and put them in a different bag.

3. Pull out one card from each bag without looking.

4. Make a sentence to match the cards you have chosen, for example:

   저는 낡은 컴퓨터가 있어요.
   **jeoneun nalgeun keompyuteo-ga isseoyo**
   (*I have an old computer.*)

5. Keep playing until all the cards have been chosen.

6. You can put the cards back in the bag and start again – each time the sentences will be different.

# Key Words

TRACK NUMBER
27

공항 **gonghang** — airport

학교 **hakgyo** — school

호텔 **hotel** — hotel

은행 **eunhaeng** — bank

박물관 **bakmulguan** — museum

식당 **sikdang** — restaurant

병원 **byeongwon** — hospital

기차역 **gichayeok** — train station

공원 **gongwon** — park

다리 **dari** — bridge

거리 **geori** — street

버스 정거장
**beoseu jeong-geo-jang** — bus stop

근처 **geuncheo** — nearby

... 어디에 있어요? *where's...?*
**... eodi-e isseoyo?**

저기에 **jeogi-e** — over there

TRACK NUMBER
28

*You are new in town and are asking a Korean friend about the facilities. Follow the prompts on your audio CD.*

**TOPIC 6:** How do I get there?

# Language Focus

⊙ ⊙ ⊙ ⊙ ⊙ Notice the Korean word for *hotel*. This is an example of a "loan" word borrowed from another language. Korean has borrowed many words, particularly from English. Look back at Topic 3. The words for *television*, *computer*, and *sandwich* are all examples of loan words.

⊙ ⊙ ⊙ ⊙ You can recognize loan words when you hear Korean, although you need to bear in mind that the pronunciation of the words may be adapted to Korean speech patterns.

# Questions and answers

Match the questions with their answers, as in the example.

은행이 어디에 있어요?　　　　　네, 식당 있어요.

근처에 식당 있어요?　　　　　공원은 학교 근처에 있어요.

근처에 호텔 있어요?　　　　　다리는 저기에 있어요.

공원이 어디에 있어요?　　　　　은행은 학교 옆에 있어요.

다리가 어디에 있어요?　　　　　네, 호텔은 기차역 앞에 있어요.

# Key Words

TRACK NUMBER
**29**

택시 **taeksi**      *taxi*      비행기 **bihaeng-gi**      *airplane*

버스 **beoseu**      *bus*      배 **bae**      *boat*

기차 **gicha**      *train*      자전거 **jajeon-geo**      *bicycle*

# Language Focus

◉ ◉ ◉ ◉ ◉ Notice that the syllable 차 **cha** can be used by itself to mean "vehicle" or "car" and it can also be used in combination.

기차 **gi-cha**      *train*
마차 **ma-cha**      *horse-drawn carriage*

◉ ◉ ◉ ◉ The particle 로 **ro** is used after a mode of transportation to mean "by."

차로 **cha-ro**  *by car*
택시로 **taeksi-ro** *by taxi*
기차로 **gicha-ro** *by train*

**TOPIC 6:** How do I get there?

# Word Square

Can you find the seven different means of transportation in the word square?
Write out the pronunciation and meaning for the words you have found, as in
the example.

| 은 | 에 | 처 | 소 | 항 | 버 | 스 | 요 |
|---|---|---|---|---|---|---|---|
| 어 | 자 | 전 | 거 | 턴 | 학 | 근 | 지 |
| 네 | 뉴 | 로 | 턴 | 에 | 다 | 캐 | 배 |
| 퓨 | 있 | 정 | 기 | 다 | 호 | 교 | 예 |
| 가 | 은 | 인 | 차 | 컴 | 퓨 | 비 | 인 |
| 택 | 시 | 자 | 의 | 에 | 버 | 행 | 탁 |
| 공 | 헨 | 크 | 기 | 리 | 다 | 기 | 자 |
| 처 | 버 | 비 | 전 | 차 | 예 | 텔 | 요 |

<u>cha</u> *(car/vehicle)*     _____

_____     _____

_____     _____

_____

# Key Words

TRACK NUMBER
30

| 실례합니다 | excuse me! | 오른쪽으로 | on the right |
| sillye-hamnida | | oreunjjo-geuro | |
| ...에 어떻게 가요? | how do I | 왼쪽으로. | on the left |
| ...-e eotteoke gayo? | get to...? | oenjjo-geuro | |
| ... 가세요 | go... | 직진 하세요 | go straight |
| ...gaseyo | | jikjin haseyo | ahead |
| | | 여기 yeogi | here |
| 첫 번째 골목 | the first | | |
| cheot beonjje golmok | street | 그리고 geurigo | then |
| 두 번째 골목 | the second | 그리고 나서 | after that |
| du beonjje golmok | street | geurigo naseo | |

TRACK NUMBER
31

*Ask for directions to places around town. Listen to the example and then follow the prompts on your audio CD.*

**TOPIC 6:** How do I get there?

# Language Focus

In the phrase ...에 어떻게 가요? **...e eotteoke gayo?** *(how do I get to...?)*, 에 **"e"** denotes the direction, 어떻게 **etteoke** means *how* and 가요 **gayo** is the verb *"go"* with the polite ending 요 **yo**. So the sentence reads *...to how go?*

> 기차역에 어떻게 가요? **gichayeog-e eotteoke gayo?**
> *How do I get to the train station?*
>
> 서울에 어떻게 가요? **seoul-e eotteoke gayo?**
> *How do I get to Seoul?*

To answer the question, you can use the verb "go" again, this time with the ending 세요 **seyo**: 가세요 **gaseyo**. 세요 **seyo** is an "honorific" ending that you cannot use when talking about yourself. You should use this honorific ending when you are giving someone directions or instructions.

> 왼쪽으로 가세요. **eonjjo-geuro gaseyo**
> *Go/Turn left.* ("on the left go")
>
> 오른쪽으로 가세요. **oreunjjo-geuro gaseyo**
> *Go/Turn right.* ("on the right go")
>
> 기차로 가세요. **gicha-ro gaseyo** *Go by train.* ("train by go")

If you want to say *Take the first street on the right*, etc. you need to use the particle 에서 **eseo** *("at")* between *"street"* and *"on the left/right."* Notice the slight change in pronunciation (**golmok/golmo-geseo**).

> 첫 번째 골목에서 왼쪽으로 가세요.
> **cheot beonjje golmo-geseo oenjjo-geuro gaseyo**
> *Take the first street on the left.* ("first street at on the left go")
>
> 두 번째 골목에서 오른쪽으로 가세요.
> **du beonjje golmo-geseo oreunjjo-geuro gaseyo**
> *Take the second street on the right.*

**TOPIC 6: How do I get there?**

# Which way?

Make questions and answers, as in the example.

실례합니다. 기차역에 어떻게 가요?
**sillye-hamnida. gicha-yeoge eotteoke gayo?**
*Excuse me, how do I get to the station?*

첫 번째 골목에서 왼쪽으로 가세요.
**cheot beonjje golmo-geseo oenjjo-geuro gaseyo**
*Take the first street on the left.*

1

2

3

4

5

6

**TOPIC 6: How do I get there?**

# Around town

Below is a plan of a small town with some landmarks shown.
Starting from *You are here*, try to give directions to the following places:

| 기차역 | 병원 | 공원 | 버스 정거장 |
|---|---|---|---|
| **gicha-yeok*** | **byeongwon** | **gongwon** | **beoseu jeong-geo-jang** |
| *the station* | *the hospital* | *the park* | *the bus stop* |

For example, your directions to the station could be something like this:

직진하세요. 그리고 첫 번째 골목에서 오른쪽으로 가세요. 기차역은 다리 근처에 있어요.
**jikjin haseyo. geurigo cheot beonjje golmo-geseo oreunjjo-geuro gaseyo. gicha-yeogeun dari geuncheo-e isseoyo.**
*Go straight ahead. Then take the first street on the right. The station is near the bridge.*

(*The final **k** in **yeok** can change to **g** when endings are added – see pronunciation tips on page 91)

# Unscramble the conversation

See if you can read the Korean in the word balloons. Then put the conversation into the correct order.

네? **a**

여기에서 왼쪽으로 가세요.
그리고 공원에서 오른쪽으로 가세요.
버스 정거장은 은행 옆에 있어요. **b**

버스 정거장이 어디예요? **c**

네, 고맙습니다. **d**

충무로에 어떻게 가요? **e**

충무로요? 버스로 가세요. **f**

실례합니다. **g**

ORDER: g,_____

Check your answer with the conversation on your audio CD.

TRACK NUMBER
**32**

# Town Planning

TRACK NUMBER
**33**

1. Cut out the pictures of places around town from Game Card 6.

2. Listen to the first set of directions for the bank on your audio CD.

3. Pause the CD and stick the picture of the bank in the correct place on the town map on your game card.

4. Listen to the next set of directions and stick down the appropriate picture.

5. Repeat for all the directions until you have all your pictures stuck down on the map.

6. Looking at the completed map, you could try to give directions to the various places yourself. For example:

두 번째 골목에서 왼쪽으로 가세요.
은행은 학교 오른쪽 옆에 있어요.
**du beonjjae golmo-geseo eonjjo-geuro gaseyo.**
**eunhaengeun hakgyo oreunjjok yeope isseoyo.**
*Take the second street on the left. The bank is on the right, next to the school.*

# Key Words

| 아내 **anae** | wife | 여동생 **yeo-dongsaeng** | younger sister ("female younger sibling") |
|---|---|---|---|
| 남편 **nampyeon** | husband | 남동생 **nam-dongsaeng** | younger brother ("male younger sibling") |
| 아이 **ai** | child | 언니 **eonni** | older sister (for female) |
| 딸 **ttal** | daughter | 누나 **nuna** | older sister (for male) |
| 아들 **adeul** | son | 오빠 **oppa** | older brother (for female) |
| 어머니 **eomeoni** | mother | 형 **hyeong** | older brother (for male) |
| 아버지 **abeoji** | father | | |

*Korean has different words for "brother" and "sister" depending on whether they are older or younger. The words for older siblings also change depending on whether <u>you</u> are male or female. This means there are six words altogether: younger sister/younger brother/older brother (for female)/older sister (for female)/older brother (for male)/older sister (for male). See Key Words panel.*

**TOPIC 7:** Who's this?

# Language Focus

⊙ ⊙ ⊙ ⊙ ⊙ You can make sentences about your family using the verbs you've already met: 있어요 -**isseoyo** *is/has* and 없어요 **eopsseoyo** *isn't/hasn't* (**see Topic 3**).

저는 언니가 있어요. **jeoneun eonni-ga isseoyo**
*I have an older sister/older sisters.* (speaking as a female)

저는 형이 없어요. **jeoneun hyeong-i eopsseoyo**
*I don't have an older brother/older brothers.* (speaking as a male)

저는 아이가 없어요. **jeoneun ai-ga eopsseoyo**
*I don't have any children.*

# What does it mean?

Join the English to the pronunciation and the Korean script, as in the example.

| English | Pronunciation | Korean |
|---|---|---|
| *child* | **nuna** | 아버지 |
| *husband* | **oppa** | 여동생 |
| *older brother* (female) | **hyeong** | 딸 |
| *daughter* | **anae** | 남동생 |
| *father* | **adeul** | 아이 |
| *mother* | **nampyeon** | 언니 |
| *older sister* (male) | **ai** | 누나 |
| *younger brother* | **ttal** | 어머니 |
| *wife* | **yeo-dongsaeng** | 오빠 |
| *older sister* (female) | **nam-dongsaeng** | 형 |
| *younger sister* | **eon-ni** | 아내 |
| *older brother* (male) | **eomeoni** | 남편 |
| *son* | **abeoji** | 아들 |

# Language Focus

⊙ ⊙ ⊙ ⊙ ⊙ Remember that Koreans generally avoid using the subject *"you"* when speaking. Instead they normally use a title (e.g., 씨 **ssi** *Mr./Mrs./Miss*) after the name or omit it altogether. In the same way, there's no need to include an equivalent of *"your."*

> 집이 어디예요? **jibi eodi-yeyo?**
> *Where is (your) house?*

> 마이클 브라운 씨, 남동생이에요?
> **maikeul beurawun-ssi, nam-dongsaeng-ieyo?**
> *Mr. Michael Brown, is it (your) younger brother?*

⊙ ⊙ ⊙ ⊙ Use 제 **je** *(my)* to say something *"belongs to me."*

> 이건 제 컴퓨터예요. **igeon je keompyuteo-yeyo**
> *This is my computer.* ("this my computer is")

> 제 어머니예요. **je eomeoni-yeyo**
> *It's my mother.* ("my mother is")

⊙ ⊙ ⊙ There is a possessive particle 의 **ui**. This is put in the same position as the English *'s:* 어머니의 책 **eomeoni-ui chaek** *(mother's book)*; 오빠의 학교 **oppa-ui hakgyo** *(older brother's school)*. However, 의 **ui** is often omitted in speech.

> 영민(의) 자전거예요. **yeongmin(-ui) jajeongeo-yeyo**
> *It's YeongMin's bicycle.*

> 딸(의) 이름이 뭐예요? **ttal(-ui) ireum-i mwo-yeyo?**
> *What's (your) daughter's name?*

⊙ ⊙ Instead of using *"his"* or *"her"* you need to say *"that person's"*: 그 사람(의) **geu saram(-ui)** – or its *"honorific"* alternative, 그 분(의) **geu bun(-ui).**

**TOPIC 7: Who's this?**

그 사람(의) 친구예요. **geu saram-(ui) chingu-yeyo**
*It's his/her (that person's) friend.*

그 분(의) 아들이에요. **geu bun-(ui) adeul-ieyo**
*It's his/her (that person's) son.*

# Family Tree

Make up sentences about this family, as in the example.

이 진희씨는 김 민수씨(의) 아내예요.
**i jinhi-ssi-neun gim minsu-ssi(-ui) anae-yeyo**
*Jinhi Lee is Minsu Gim's wife.*

김 민수    이 진희

영철    수진

# Robert's family

Listen to Robert answering questions about his family.
Circle the correct names on the family tree, as in the example.

팀
마크
로버트

리사
사라
헨렌

켄
진희
(로버트)

영철
마크
진희

# Questions and answers

Now read the questions on the left and then match them to the answers on the right that Robert gave, as in the example.

| | |
|---|---|
| 형 있어요? | 제 어머니 이름은 사라예요. |
| 어머니 이름이 뭐예요? | 아니오, 누나 없어요. |
| 누나 있어요? | 아버지 이름은 팀이에요. |
| 형 이름이 뭐예요? | 저는 미국 시카고에서 왔어요. |
| 아버지 이름이 뭐예요? | 저는 로버트예요. |
| 이름이 뭐예요? | 형 이름은 마크예요. |
| 어디에서 왔어요? | 네, 있어요. |

**TOPIC 7:** Who's this?

# Language Focus

To ask someone politely *"who's this?"* use the phrase 이 분은 누구세요? **i bun-eun nuguseyo?**. 이 분 **i bun** is the honorific way of saying *"this person"* (see page 66 for *"that person"*), and 누구세요 **nuguseyo** is a combination of 누구? **nugu?** *(who?)* and the honorific ending 세요 **seyo**.

> 이 분은 누구세요? **i bun-eun nuguseyo?** *Who's this?*
>
> 제 누나예요. **je nuna-yeyo** *It's my sister.*
>
> 제 친구, 신 민선씨예요. **je chingu, sin minseon-ssi-yeyo**
> *It's my friend, Mrs./Miss Minseon Sin.*

When introducing a sibling, you don't need to use the title with the name. But if introducing a senior member of the family, such as parents or grandparents, Koreans wouldn't normally give names at all, but instead use the honorific ending 세요 **seyo**, for example 제 아버지세요 **je abeoji-seyo** *It's my father.*

Look at this conversation.

> – 안녕하세요, 상준씨? **annyeong-haseyo, sangjun-ssi**
> *Hello, Sangjun.*
>
> – 안녕하세요, 제인씨. 이 분은 누구세요? **annyeong-haseyo, jein-ssi. i bun-eun nuguseyo?** *Hello, Jane. Who's this?*
>
> – 제 남동생 마크예요. **je nam-dongsaeng makeu-yeyo**
> *This is my younger brother, Mark.*
>
> – 만나서 반갑습니다, 마크씨. **mannaseo bangap-seumnida, makeu-ssi** *Pleased to meet you, Mark.*
>
> – 만나서 반갑습니다, 상준씨. **mannaseo bangap-seumnida, sangjun-ssi** *Pleased to meet you, Sangjun.*

TRACK NUMBER
**36**

Now introduce <u>your</u> family using the conversation above as a guide. Follow the prompts on your audio CD.

# Key Words

TRACK NUMBER
37

| | | | | | |
|---|---|---|---|---|---|
| 하나 **hana** | one | | 일곱 **ilgop** | seven |
| 둘 **dul** | two | | 여덟 **yeodeol** | eight |
| 셋 **set** | three | | 아홉 **ahop** | nine |
| 넷 **net** | four | | 열 **yeol** | ten |
| 다섯 **daseot** | five | | 열하나 **yeol-hana** | eleven |
| 여섯 **yeoseot** | six | | 열둘 **yeol-dul** | twelve |

# Language Focus

◎ ◎ ◎ ◎ ◎ There are two sets of numbers in Korean. Above are the "pure" Korean ones. An alternative "Sino" set of numbers exists borrowed from the Chinese language (e.g., one = 일 **il**, two = 이 **i**). However, as a beginner you can start with the Korean set.

◎ ◎ ◎ ◎ If you are using the numbers in the abstract, they can be used as above. But if you want to count things or people, you have to include a "classifier." Classifiers are put after the number and are similar to words in English such as *a bar* (of chocolate), *a roll* (of film). The most common classifier is 개 **gae** ("thing"), but when you count people you need to use either 명 **myeong** (plain) or 분 **bun** (honorific).

> 아이 다섯 명 **ai daseot-myeong** *five children.*
> 펜 열여섯 개 **pen yeol-yeoseot gae** *16 ("ten-six") pens*

◎ ◎ ◎ The spelling of the numbers one to four changes slightly when a classifier is used:
하나 **hana** → 한 **han**; 둘 **dul** → 두 **du**; 셋 **set** → 세 **se**; 넷 **net** → 네 **ne**.

> 저는 펜이 두 개 있어요. **jeoneun pen-i du gae isseoyo**
> *I have two pens.*
> 저는 언니가 세 명 있어요. **jeoneun eonni-ga se myeong isseoyo** *I have three older sisters.*

**TOPIC 7:** Who's this?

# How many?

Match the numbers to the pronunciation, as in the example.

| | |
|---|---|
| 하나 | dul |
| 둘 | daseot |
| 셋 | yeoseot |
| 넷 | yeol |
| 다섯 | ahop |
| 여섯 | set |
| 일곱 | ilgop |
| 여덟 | hana |
| 아홉 | yeodeol |
| 열 | net |

# Korean sums

Circle the correct answer to these sums, as in the example.

1  하나 + 넷 = 하나 둘 셋 넷 (다섯) 여섯 일곱 여덟 아홉 열 열하나 열둘

2  둘 + 여섯 = 하나 둘 셋 넷 다섯 여섯 일곱 여덟 아홉 열 열하나 열둘

3  셋 X 둘 = 하나 둘 셋 넷 다섯 여섯 일곱 여덟 아홉 열 열하나 열둘

4  아홉 + 셋 = 하나 둘 셋 넷 다섯 여섯 일곱 여덟 아홉 열 열하나 열둘

5  열둘 − 열 = 하나 둘 셋 넷 다섯 여섯 일곱 여덟 아홉 열 열하나 열둘

6  여덟 + 둘 = 하나 둘 셋 넷 다섯 여섯 일곱 여덟 아홉 열 열하나 열둘

7  다섯 − 셋 = 하나 둘 셋 넷 다섯 여섯 일곱 여덟 아홉 열 열하나 열둘

8  열하나 − 열 = 하나 둘 셋 넷 다섯 여섯 일곱 여덟 아홉 열 열하나 열둘

9  셋 X 셋 = 하나 둘 셋 넷 다섯 여섯 일곱 여덟 아홉 열 열하나 열둘

**TOPIC 7: Who's this?**

# My family

Use the table below to make sentences about yourself, as in the examples.

저는 누나가 두 명 있어요. **jeoneun nuna-ga du myeong isseoyo** *I have two older sisters.*
저는 아들이 없어요. **jeoneun adeul-i eopsseoyo** *I don't have any sons.*

저는
**jeoneun**

언니/누나
**eonni/nuna**

오빠/형
**oppa/hyeong**

(남/여)동생
**(yeo-/nam-)dongsaeng**

아들 **adeul**

딸 **ttal**

아이 **ai**

가 **-ga**

이 **-i**

한 명
**han myeong**

두 명
**du myeong**

세 명
**se myeong**

있어요 **isseoyo**

없어요 **eopsseoyo**

# Listen and speak

Now imagine you are with some of your family looking for the station and you meet a Korean friend.

Prepare carefully the information below you will need to take part in the conversation. Then go to your audio CD and see how you get on introducing your family.

1 Think of two members of your family – one male and one female. For example, your husband and your daughter; or your brother and your mother.

2 How would you tell someone their names in Korean?

3 How would you ask *How do I get to the station?*

4 How do you say *thank you* and *goodbye*?

You can repeat the conversation, but this time use two different members of your family and ask how to get to the bus stop.

**TOPIC 7:** Who's this?

# Bingo!

1. Cut out the small number tokens and the bingo cards on Game Card 7.

2. Find 16 buttons for each player or make 16 small blank pieces of card (to cover the squares on the bingo card).

3. Put the tokens into a bag and shake thoroughly.

4. Pull out a number token and say the number out loud in Korean.

5. If you have that number on your card, cover the square with a button or blank piece of card. If you have more than one square with that number, you can only cover one.

6. Put the number token back in the bag and shake again.

7. Repeat steps 3–6 until you have all the squares covered on the bingo card. Then you can shout: 이겼다! **igyeotta!** (*I've won!*)

You can play with a friend or challenge yourself.

# Key Words

TRACK NUMBER
39

교사 **gyo-sa**     *teacher*     운전사 **unjeon-sa**     *driver*

학생 **haksaeng**     *student*     회사원 **hoesawon**     *office worker*

의사 **ui-sa**     *doctor*     점원 **jeomwon**     *store assistant*

요리사 **yori-sa**     *chef*     엔지니어 **enjinieo**     *engineer*

회계사 **hoegye-sa**     *accountant*     배우 **bae-u**     *actor*

*If your occupation or those of your family aren't listed here, try to find out what they are in Korean.*

**TOPIC 8: What do you do?**

# What does it mean?

Join the Korean to the pronunciation and the English, as in the example.

| 의사 | yori-sa | office worker |
| 점원 | hoegye-sa | accountant |
| 요리사 | jeomwon | actor |
| 회계사 | gyo-sa | driver |
| 교사 | haksaeng | store assistant |
| 배우 | ui-sa | engineer |
| 학생 | enjinieo | doctor |
| 운전사 | bae-u | chef |
| 엔지니어 | unjeon-sa | teacher |
| 회사원 | hoesawon | student |

# The tools of the trade

Match the jobs to the tools of the trade, as in the example.

엔지니어

학생

의사

회계사

요리사

운전사

배우

# Language Focus

⊙ ⊙ ⊙ ⊙ ⊙ ⊙ The Korean for *"job"* is easy to remember: 직업 **jigeop**. To make a question, just add 뭐예요? **mwo-yeyo?** *(what?)*.

> 직업이 뭐예요? **jigeop-i mwo-yeyo?** *What's your job?*

⊙ ⊙ ⊙ ⊙ ⊙ The answer is simple: just use 저는 **jeoneun** + job + 이에요/예요 **-ieyo/-yeyo**.

> 저는 회사원이에요. **jeoneun hoesawon-ieyo**
> *I'm an office worker.*
>
> 저는 학생이에요. **jeoneun haksaeng-ieyo**
> *I'm a student.*
>
> 저는 배우예요. **jeoneun baeu-yeyo**
> *I'm an actor.*

⊙ ⊙ ⊙ Other useful phrases include:

> 퇴직 했어요. **toejik haesseoyo**
> *I'm retired.*
>
> 직업이 없어요. **jigeobi eopsseoyo**
> *I don't have a job at the moment.*
>
> 집에서 일해요. **jibeseo il-haeyo**
> *I work from home.*

**TOPIC 8:** What do you do?

# Listen and note

TRACK NUMBER
40

Listen to two people telling you about themselves
and fill out the details in English on the forms below.

First name: .....Chanho.........................

Family name:...............................................

Nationality: ...............................................

Name of spouse: .......................................

No. of children: .........................................

Occupation: ...............................................

First name: ...............................................

Family name:...............................................

Nationality: ...............................................

Name of spouse: .......................................

No. of children: .........................................

Occupation: ...............................................

# Your turn to speak

TRACK NUMBER
41

Now you give same information about yourself.
Follow the prompts on your audio CD.

# What's the answer?

Match the questions to the answers.
For example: **1d**

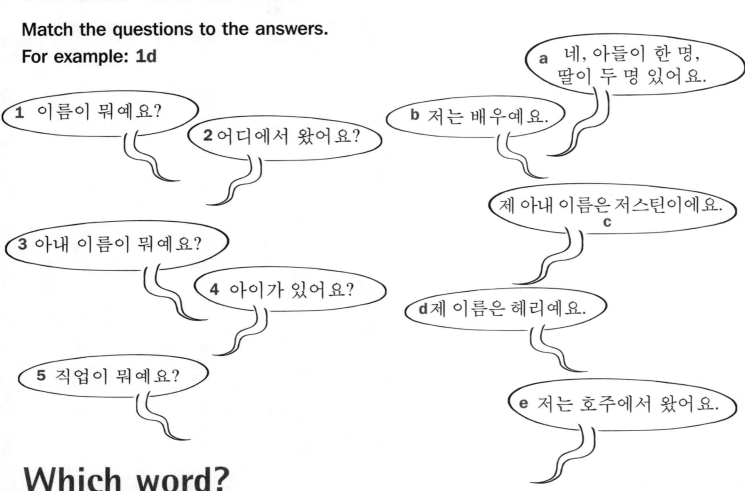

1 이름이 뭐예요?

2 어디에서 왔어요?

3 아내 이름이 뭐예요?

4 아이가 있어요?

5 직업이 뭐예요?

a 네, 아들이 한 명, 딸이 두 명 있어요.

b 저는 배우예요.

c 제 아내 이름은 저스틴이에요.

d 제 이름은 헤리예요.

e 저는 호주에서 왔어요.

# Which word?

Write the correct number of the word in the box to complete the description, as in the example.

제 __3__ 은 헤리예요. 저는 _____ 입니다. 저는 호주 멜본에서 왔어요. 제 _____ 이름은 저스틴이에요. 그리고 저는 _____ 가 세 명 있어요. _____ 한 명, 딸 _____ 있어요.

| | | |
|---|---|---|
| 1 아내 | 2 아들 | 3 이름 |
| 4 아이 | 5 두 명 | 6 배우 |

**TOPIC 8: What do you do?**

# Key Words

TRACK NUMBER
42

| | | | | | |
|---|---|---|---|---|---|
| 공장 **gongjang** | *factory* | | 대학교 **daehakgyo** | *college* |
| 가게 **gage** | *store* | | 회사 **hoesa** | *company* |
| 극장 **geukjang** | *theater* | | | |
| 사무실 **samusil** | *office* | | | |

*Look back as well at the Key Words on page 54 for other places of work.*

# Language Focus

To say where you work use the particle 에서 **eseo** *(at)* with the verb 일해요 **il-haeyo**, meaning *work*.

> 저는 의사예요. 병원에서 일해요.
> **jeoneun uisa-yeyo. byeongwon-eseo il-haeyo**
> *I'm a doctor. I work in a hospital.*

To say where the place of work is, you need to add 에 있는 **e in-neun** after the name of the town or country: *town/country* + **e in-neun** + *place of work* + **eseo** + **il-haeyo**.

> 부산에 있는 큰 회사에서 일해요.
> **busan-e in-neun keun hoesa-eseo il-haeyo**
> *I work for a large company in Busan.*

To ask where someone works use 어디? **eodi** *(where?)* with 일해요 **il-haeyo** or its honorific form 일하세요 **il-haseyo** to show more deference.

> 어디에서 일해요/일하세요?
> **eodi-eseo il-haeyo/il-haseyo?**
> *Where do you work? ("where at work?")*

**TOPIC 8:** What do you do?

# Word Square

Can you find the eight different work-places in the word square?
Words can read horizontally or vertically.

Write out the meaning for the words you have found.

*factory*

| 병 | 명 | 처 | 공 | 장 | 버 | 니 | 학 |
|---|---|---|---|---|---|---|---|
| 원 | 입 | 틴 | 거 | 턴 | 있 | 근 | 교 |
| 은 | 뉴 | 가 | 턴 | 식 | 당 | 캐 | 요 |
| 사 | 무 | 실 | 는 | 다 | 는 | 교 | 멜 |
| 멜 | 입 | 인 | 차 | 주 | 입 | 극 | 인 |
| 택 | 가 | 자 | 주 | 에 | 버 | 장 | 탁 |
| 공 | 게 | 크 | 교 | 리 | 다 | 기 | 자 |
| 주 | 제 | 비 | 교 | 은 | 행 | 제 | 요 |

_____

_____

_____

_____

_____

_____

Now make sentences for each of the work-places, as in the example:

저는 엔지니어예요. 공장에서 일 해요.

**jeoneun enjinieo-yeyo. gongjang-eseo il haeyo.**

*I'm an engineer. I work in a factory.*

# What are they saying?

Match the people with what they are saying. For example: 1e

**1** 저는 인천에 있는 레스토랑에서 일 해요.

**4** 저는 캐나다에 있는 공장에서 일 해요.

**2** 저는 영국에 있는 학교에서 일 해요.

**5** 저는 미국 은행에서 일 해요.

**3** 저는 아일랜드에 있는 극장에서 일 해요.

**6** 저는 부산에 있는 가게에서 일 해요.

a

b

c

d

e

f

## ACTIVITIES

# Listen and speak

Imagine you are a chef. You're meeting someone for the first time and they are asking you about yourself.

Prepare carefully the information below you will need to take part in the conversation. Then go to your audio CD and see how you get on talking about yourself.

1 Your name is Byeongsu Kim (김 병수).

2 You're from Busan.

3 You're a chef.

4 You work in a Korean restaurant in New York.

5 You have two daughters.

6 Your wife is a teacher in a big school.

# Which word?

Now write the correct number of the word in the box to complete the description of Byeongsu's life, as in the example.

| 1 대학교 | 2 요리사 | 3 학교에서 | 4 아내 |
|---|---|---|---|
| 5 예요 | 6 일 해요 | 7 딸 | 8 근처 |

제 이름은 김 병수 __5__ 저는 _____예요. 한국 부산에서 왔어요.

저는 뉴욕에 있는 한국 식당에서 _____. 제 _____ 는 선생님이에요.

식당 _____ 에 있는 아주 큰 _____ 일 해요.

저희는 _____ 이 두 명 있어요. 둘 다 _____ 학생이에요.

**TOPIC 8:** What do you do?

# Where do I work?

1. Tear out the work-place picture cards and profession word cards on Game Card 8.

2. Turn the cards face down on a table, with the pictures on one end of the table and the words on the other.

3. Turn a word card and make a sentence with the profession as appropriate, e.g. 저는 교사예요. **jeoneun gyosa-yeyo** *(I'm a teacher).*

4. Then turn a picture card. If the work-place picture matches the profession, say 저는 ... 에서 일 해요. **jeoneun ...-eseo il haeyo** *(I work in a/an ...)*, e.g. 저는 학교에서 일 해요. **jeoneun hakgyo-eseo il haeyo** *(I work in a school).*

5. If you turn a matching picture and say both sentences correctly, you get to keep the cards. If you don't, you must turn the cards face down and try again.

6. The winner is the one who collects the most cards.

7. You can compete with a friend or challenge yourself against the clock.

*(Review the vocabulary on pages 54, 56 and 74*

○ ○ ○ ○ ○ This **Test Yourself** section reviews all the Korean you have learned in this program. Have a go at the activities. If you find you have forgotten something, go back to the relevant topic(s) and look again at the **Key Words** and **Language Focus** panels.

# May I have...?

Ask for the following, as in the example:

 차 주세요.
**cha juseyo**

1

2

3

4

5

6

# Listen and check

Listen to Jinhi talking about herself and decide if the
following sentences are true or false.

TRACK NUMBER
44

|  |  | True | False |
|---|---|---|---|
| 1 | Jinhi is Korean. | ☐ | ☐ |
| 2 | She comes from a small town. | ☐ | ☐ |
| 3 | She's a teacher. | ☐ | ☐ |
| 4 | She works in France. | ☐ | ☐ |
| 5 | Her husband is an engineer. | ☐ | ☐ |
| 6 | She has five children. | ☐ | ☐ |

# Which word?

Now write the correct number of the word in the box to
complete the description of Jinhi, as in the example.

| 1 큰 | 2 남편 | 3 한 명 | 4 병원 |
|---|---|---|---|
| 5 아이 | 6 딸 | 7 한국 | 8 교사 |

저는 박 진희예요. _7_ 에 있는 ____ 도시 인천에서 왔어요.

저는 ____ 예요. 영국에 있는 작은 한국학교에서 일 해요.

제 ____ 은 의사예요. 한국학교 옆에 있는 큰 ____ 에서 일 해요.

저희는 ____ 가 네 명 있어요. 아들 ____ 그리고 ____ 이 세 명이에요.

Can you try and make up a similar description about yourself?

# Read and check

Look at the picture and decide if the sentences are true or false.
Look back at topics 4–6 if you are unsure of any of the words.

|  | True | False |
|---|:---:|:---:|
| 1 그림에 은행이 있어요. | ☐ | ☐ |
| 2 병원이 은행의 오른쪽 옆에 있어요. | ☐ | ☐ |
| 3 학교가 은행의 왼쪽 옆에 있어요. | ☐ | ☐ |
| 4 골목에 개가 있어요. | ☐ | ☐ |
| 5 골목에 차가 없어요. | ☐ | ☐ |
| 6 차 위에 작은 고양이가 있어요. | ☐ | ☐ |
| 7 학교 뒤에 큰 나무가 있어요. | ☐ | ☐ |
| 8 병원 앞에 낡은 자전거가 있어요. | ☐ | ☐ |

# What does it mean?

Can you remember these words? Join the words and write the pronunciation next to the Korean, as in the example

| | | |
|---|---|---|
| children | 딸 | _____ |
| husband | 아들 | _____ |
| son | 어머니 | _____ |
| daughter | 아이 | *ai* |
| father | 형 | _____ |
| mother | 여동생 | _____ |
| younger sister | 아내 | _____ |
| older brother (to a male) | 남편 | _____ |
| older sister (to a female) | 남동생 | _____ |
| wife | 언니 | _____ |
| younger brother | 아버지 | _____ |

# How do you say it?

Now see if you can say these in Korean, as in the example.

1  *My husband is a doctor.*
   제 남편은 의사예요.
   **je nampyeon-eun uisa-yeyo**

2  *I have a younger sister.*

3  *My son is an engineer.*

4  *Jinhi's mother is from Daejeon.*

5  *My wife's name is Claire.*

6  *My older brother is an actor.*

7  *I don't have any children.*

8  *I have three daughters.*

# At the tourist information office

TRACK NUMBER
45

Finally, you are going to test your new Korean conversational skills by joining in the dialog on your audio CD.

You're going to ask for some information at a tourist information office.

To prepare, first see if you can remember these words and phrases. Write the pronunciation and English next to the Korean, as in the example.

안녕히 가세요    **annyeonghi gaseyo** _goodbye_ (to s.o. leaving)

안녕히 계세요    _____

안녕하세요    _____

고맙습니다    _____

뒤    _____

오른쪽    _____

왼쪽    _____

버스    _____

근처    _____

큰    _____

박물관    _____

어디?    _____

Now follow the prompts on your audio CD. Don't worry if you don't manage everything the first time around. Just keep repeating it until you are fluent.

◎ ◎ ◎ ◎ ◎    Congratulations on successfully completing this introductory _Read and Speak Korean for Beginners_ program. You have overcome the obstacle of learning a new language in an unfamiliar script. You should now have the confidence to enjoy using the Korean you have learned. You have also acquired a sound basis from which to expand your language skills in whichever direction you choose. Good luck!

This Reference section gives an overview of the Korean script and pronunciation. You can use it to refer to as you work your way through the *Read and Speak Korean for Beginners* program. Don't expect to take it all in from the beginning. The program is designed to build your confidence step by step as you progress through the topics. The details will start to fall into place gradually as you become more familiar with the Korean characters and language.

# The Korean script

The Korean script, more properly called the Hangeul script, is not nearly as difficult as it might seem at first glance. Although Korean used to be written in Chinese characters (Hanja), these are now only rarely used and everyday material is written in the Hangeul alphabet developed in the 15th century.

The main difference between the way Hangeul is written and most other scripts, is that each syllable of a word in written together to form a square shape – the written shape most familiar to most 15th-century Koreans.

## The alphabet: consonants

There are 14 consonants (non-vowels) in the Hangeul alphabet, plus five double letters.

Here are the consonants with their pronunciation. Where a letter has two pronunciations shown, these alternatives are used at the beginning or end of a syllable – see page 90 for more detail.

| ㄱ | ㄴ | ㄷ | ㄹ | ㅁ | ㅂ | ㅅ | ㅇ | ㅈ | ㅊ | ㅋ | ㅌ | ㅍ | ㅎ |
|---|---|---|---|---|---|---|---|---|---|---|---|---|---|
| g/k | n | d/t | r/l | m | b/p | s/t | -/ng | j/t | ch/t | k | t | p | h |

Here are the five double consonants.

| ㄲ | ㄸ | ㅃ | ㅆ | ㅉ |
|---|---|---|---|---|
| kk/t | tt | pp | ss/t | jj |

# The alphabet: vowels and diphthongs

⊙ ⊙ ⊙ ⊙ ⊙ There are ten vowels in the Hangeul alphabet, plus a number of diphthongs (vowel combinations). Here are ten main vowels with their pronunciation.

| ㅏ | ㅑ | ㅓ | ㅕ | ㅗ | ㅛ | ㅜ | ㅠ | ㅡ | ㅣ |
|---|---|---|---|---|---|---|---|---|---|
| a | ya | eo | yeo | o | yo | u | yu | eu | i |

⊙ ⊙ ⊙ ⊙ Here are the diphthongs. You will quickly start to recognize the most common.

| ㅐ | ㅔ | ㅒ | ㅖ | ㅘ | ㅝ | ㅙ | ㅚ | ㅞ | ㅟ | ㅢ |
|---|---|---|---|---|---|---|---|---|---|---|
| ae | e | yae | ye | wa | wo | wae | oe | we | wi | ui |

# Syllables

⊙ ⊙ ⊙ ⊙ ⊙ Korean words are made up of one or more syllables. The syllables are composed of the letters written in a square shape according to certain rules. It is useful to be familiar with these rules, but don't worry about trying to memorize them at this point.

⊙ ⊙ ⊙ ⊙ A syllable has to start with a consonant (which can be the silent consonant ㅇ – see pronunciation). There are two, or occasionally three, consonants, but only one vowel (diphthongs included).

⊙ ⊙ ⊙ If the vowel is written with a vertical line, it is placed to the right of the consonant; if with a horizontal line, it is placed under the consonant. If both lines appear, the consonant is placed in the top left quarter. The second (and third consonants) are always placed at the bottom (with the third consonant to the right of the second).

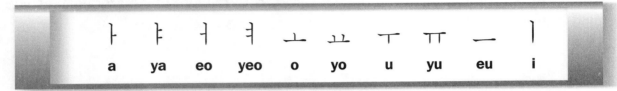

ㄴ n + ㅏ a = 나 na

ㅅ s + ㅟ wi = 쉬 swi

ㅂ b + ㅗ o + ㅁ m = 봄 bom

ㅎ h + ㅘ wa + ㄹ l = 활 hwal

ㅇ - + ㅏ a + ㄴ n + ㅈ j = 앉 an(j)

# Pronunciation

Some elements of Korean pronunciation need special attention.

The consonants shown with two alternative pronunciations on page 89 (except **r/l**) are pronounced as the first alternative when they are the initial consonant in a syllable, and as the second alternative for a final consonant.

가요 **gayo** *go*          국 **guk** *soup*

일본 **ilbon** *Japan*          밥 **bap** *rice/food*

When ㄹ **r/l** is surrounded by vowels "**r**" is pronounced. Otherwise, "**l**" is pronounced.

나라 **nara** *country*          서울 **seoul** *Seoul*

ㅅ **s** is pronounced "**sh**" when followed by the vowels ㅑ, ㅕ, ㅛ, ㅠ or ㅣ.

신 **shin** *Shin* (surname)          쇼 **shyo** *show*

Note also that the final consonants "**t**" and "**k**" are not pronounced strongly and that double consonants (see page 89) sound much tighter than the single equivalents.

When the letter ㅇ is the first consonant it is silent. Only the vowel sound is pronounced. When the second consonant, it is pronounced "**ng**" as in *song*.

아버지 **abeoji** *father*          은행 **eunhaeng** *bank*

The three letters ㄱ, ㄷ, and ㅂ are half aspirated and half voiced, and sound somewhere between **g, d, b** and **k, t, p**.

Some Korean vowels sound very similar. ㅔ **e** and ㅐ **ae** are both pronounced **ae** as in *bare*; ㅖ **ye** and ㅒ **yae** are both pronounced **yae** as in *yeah*; ㅞ **we**, ㅙ **wae** and ㅚ **oe** are all pronounced **wae** as in *where*.

When certain syllables combine in a word, there can be changes to the pronunciation. This is known as "linking." Two important changes are:

- When the consonant ㅂ **b/p** is followed by the consonant ㄴ **n**, the ㅂ **b/p** is pronounced **m**. For example, in the word for *thank you:* 고맙습니다 **gomap-seumnida** (not **gomap-seupnida**).

- When a syllable within a word begins with the silent ㅇ, the final consonant of the previous syllable replaces the silent ㅇ. If this is one of the consonants with alternative initial and final pronunciations (see above), it will be pronounced with its *initial* sound. For example, 이것 **igeot** *(this)* + 이 **i** *(as for)* = 이거시 **igeosi**.

TRACK NUMBER
1

You will find an introduction to the sounds of Korean on track 1 of your audio.

## Topic 1

### Page 6

Check your answers with the Key Words panel on page 5.

### Page 8: What are they saying?

### Page 8: What do you hear?

You should have ticked boxes 1 and 3.

### Page 10: What does it mean?

1b, 2c, 3e, 4f, 5a, 6d

### Page 10: Which word?

안녕 __2__.

__5__하세요.

__4__최 진만이에요. 이름이__3__?

김수정__1__.

### Page 11: What are their names?

| 사라 | _Sarah (sara)_ | 팀 | _Tim (tim)_ |
| 헨렌 | _Helen (hellen)_ | 켄 | _Ken (ken)_ |
| 메리 | _Mary (meri)_ | 마크 | _Mark (makeu)_ |
| 리사 | _Lisa (lisa)_ | 로버트 | _Robert (robeoteu)_ |

### Page 12: In or out?

IN: Sarah, Sujin, Tim, Minjun, Yeongcheol

OUT: Raj, Michael, Helen, Robert, Jinhi

## Topic 2

### Page 15: Where are the countries?

캐나다 __1__  아일랜드 __3__ 영국 __4__  중국 __5__

일본 __6__  한국 __7__  호주 __8__  미국 __2__

### Page 16: How do you say it?

Check your answers with the Key Words panel on page 14.

### Page 16: Which city?

| 런던 | __London__ |
| 부산 | __Busan__ |
| 시드니 | __Sydney__ |
| 워싱턴 | __Washington__ |
| 서울 | __Seoul__ |
| 로스 엔젤레스 | __Los Angeles__ |
| 뉴욕 | __New York__ |

### Page 17: Audio track 8

Jinhi Park: Korea; Michael: America; Kyoko: Japan; Jane: England; Wangming: China; Ken: Canada

### Page 18: Where are they from?

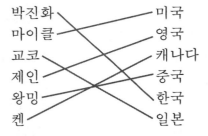

### Page 20: Who's from where?

1 피터씨는 미국 뉴욕에서 왔어요.
**piteossi-neun miguk nyuyok-eseo wasseoyo**

2 교코씨는 일본 오사카에서 왔어요.
**gyokossi-neun ilbon osaka-eseo wasseoyo**

3 헨렌씨는 캐나다 밴쿠버에서 왔어요.
**hellenssi-neun caenada baenkubeo-eseo wasseoyo**

4 마크씨는 호주 멜본에서 왔어요.
**makeussi-neun hoju melbon-eseo wasseoyo**

5 메리씨는 아일랜드 더블린에서 왔어요.
**merissi-neun ail-landeu deobeulin-eseo wasseoyo**

6 수진씨는 한국 부산에서 왔어요.
**sujinssi-neun hanguk busan-eseo wasseoyo**
7 왕밍씨는 중국 베이징에서 왔어요.
**wangmingssi-neun jungguk beijing-eseo wasseoyo**
8 팀씨는 영국 런던에서 왔어요.
**timssi-neun yeongguk leondeon-eseo wasseoyo**

## Page 21: Listen and Check

1 False; 2 True; 3 True; 4 False; 5 False

## Page 21: What does it mean?

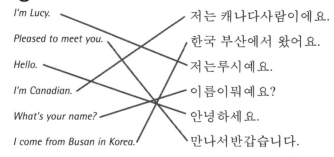

## Page 22: What does it mean?

1 저는 루시예요. **I'm Lucy.**
2 저는 캐나다사람이에요. **I'm Canadian.**
3 수진씨는 한국사람이에요. **Sujin is Korean.**
4 이름이 뭐예요? **What's your name?**
5 저는 박진희예요. **I'm Jinhi Park.**
6 팀씨는 어디에서 왔어요? **Where is Tim from?**
7 팀씨는 영국에서 왔어요. **Tim is from England.**
8 헨렌씨는 미국에서 왔어요. **Helen is from America.**

# Topic 3
## Page 25

Check your answers with the Key Words panel on page 24.

## Page 26: Word Square

computer, sofa, magazine, telephone, bag, table, chair, television

## Page 26: Odd One Out

탁자 * 의자 * 소파 * (이름)
한국 * (전화) * 호주 * 일본
(사람) * 책 * 텔레비전 * 잡지
(창문) * 수진 * 진희 * 사라
고맙습니다 * 천만예요 * (컴퓨터) * 안녕하세요

## Page 28: What's this?

1e, 2b, 3f, 4c, 5h, 6d, 7a, 8g

## Page 30: Who orders what?

Customer 1: green tea & rice cakes; Customer 2: coffee & sandwich; Customer 3: coffee & cake; Customer 4: green tea & vegetables; Customer 5: coffee & rice cakes

## Page 31: Unscramble the conversation

g, a, e, c, f, h, d, b

# Topic 4
## Page 35: What does it mean?

Check your answers with the Key Words panel on page 34.

## Page 35: What can you see?

침대 ☑ 가방 ☑
의자 ☑ 개 ☐
나무 ☐ 냉장고 ☐
그림 ☑ 고양이 ☑
탁자 ☑ 방 ☑
소파 ☐ 컴퓨터 ☑
커튼 ☑ 펜 ☑
잡지 ☐ 가스레인지 ☐
차 ☐ 책 ☑

## Page 37: Which word?

1 앞에; 2 밑에; 3 위에; 4 위에; 5 옆에; 6 밑에; 7 안에

## Page 39: Where are the mice

There are many possible sentences.
If you can, check yours with a native speaker.

## Page 41: True or False?
1 True; 2 False; 3 False; 4 False; 5 True; 6 True; 7 False;
8 True; 9 True; 10 True

# Topic 5
## Page 45: Can you remember?
Check your answers with the Key Words panel on page 44.

## Page 46: What does it mean?
새 소파    (a) new sofa
작은 커피    (a) small coffee
작은 개    (a) small dog
낡은 차    (an) old car
큰 나무    (a) big tree
작은 쥐    (a) small mouse
큰 샌드위치    (a) big sandwich
비싼 그림    (an) expensive picture

## Page 47: Listen and check
1 True; 2 False; 3 True; 4 False; 5 False

## Page 47: Unscramble the sentences
1 b, c, a;   2 b, c, a;   3 a, c, b;   4 c, a, b

## Page 50: Which word?
1 머리; 2 나무; 3 배; 4 입; 5 손가락;
6 꼬리; 7 귀; 8 코; 9 눈; 10 팔

## Page 51: At the circus
철수는 눈이 ___5___ . ___1___ 가 커요.
그리고 손에 ___6___ 가방이 있어요.

순희는 코가 ___2___ . ___4___ 이 작아요.
그리고 작은 ___3___ 가 있어요.

## Page 52: What does it look like?
There are many possible sentences.
If you can, check yours with a native speaker.

# Topic 6
## Page 55: Questions and answers
은행이 어디에 있어요?   네, 식당 있어요.
근처에 식당 있어요?   공원은 학교 근처에 있어요.
근처에 호텔 있어요?   다리는 저기에 있어요.
공원이 어디에 있어요?   은행은 학교 옆에 있어요.
다리가 어디에 있어요?   네, 호텔은 기차역 앞에 있어요.

## Page 57:
## Word Square
cha (car/vehicle)
beosen (bus)
jajeon-geo (bicycle)
bae (boat)
gicha (train)
taeksi (taxi)
bihaeng-gi (airplane)

| 은 | 에 | 처 | 소 | 항 | 버 | 스 | 요 |
|---|---|---|---|---|---|---|---|
| 어 | 자 | 전 | 거 | 턴 | 학 | 근 | 지 |
| 네 | 뉴 | 로 | 턴 | 에 | 다 | 캐 | 배 |
| 퓨 | 있 | 정 | 기 | 다 | 호 | 교 | 예 |
| 가 | 은 | 인 | 차 | 컴 | 퓨 | 비 | 인 |
| 택 | 시 | 자 | 의 | 에 | 버 | 행 | 타 |
| 공 | 헨 | 크 | 기 | 리 | 다 | 기 | 자 |
| 처 | 버 | 비 | 전 | 차 | 예 | 텔 | 요 |

## Page 60: Which way?
1 실례합니다. 버스 정거장에 어떻게 가요? **sillye-hamnida.**
   **beoseu jeong-geo-jang-e eotteoke gayo?**
   직진하세요. **jikjin-haseyo**
2 실례합니다. 기차역에 어떻게 가요? **sillye-hamnida.**
   **gicha-yeoge eotteoke gayo?**
   첫 번째 골목에서 오른쪽으로 가세요.
   **cheot beonjje golmo-geseo oreunjjo-geuro gaseyo**
3 실례합니다. 은행에 어떻게 가요? **sillye-hamnida.**
   **eunhaenge eotteoke gayo?**
   첫 번째 골목에서 왼쪽으로 가세요.
   **cheot beonjje golmo-geseo oenjjo-geuro gaseyo**
4 실례합니다. 호텔에 어떻게 가요? **sillye-hamnida.**
   **hotele eotteoke gayo?**
   두 번째 골목에서 오른쪽으로 가세요.
   **du beonjje golmo-geseo oreunjjo-geuro gaseyo**
5 실례합니다. 박물관에 어떻게 가요? **sillye-hamnida.**
   **bangmulguane eotteoke gayo?**
   버스로 가세요. **beoseuro gaseyo**
6 실례합니다. 공항에 어떻게 가요? **sillye-hamnida.**
   **gonghange eotteoke gayo?**
   기차로 가세요. **gicharo gaseyo**

## Page 61: Around town

These are model answers. Yours may vary slightly.

*the hospital:*

직진하세요. 병원은 오른쪽에 있어요.

**jikjin-haseyo. byeongwon-eun oreunjjoge isseoyo**

*the park:*

직진하세요. 그리고 첫 번째 골목에서 왼쪽으로 가세요. 공원은 학교 옆에 있어요.

**jikjin-haseyo. geurigo cheot beonjje golmo-geseo oen-jjo-geuro gaseyo. gongwon-eun hakgyo yeope isseoyo**

*the bus stop:*

직진 하세요. 그리고 첫 번째 골목에서 왼쪽으로 가세요. 버스 정거장은 오른쪽에 있어요.

**jikjin-haseyo. geurigo cheot beonjje golmo-geseo oen-jjo-geuro gaseyo. beoseu jeong-geo-jang-eun oreun-jjoge isseoyo**

## Page 62: Unscramble the conversation

g, a, e, f, c, b, d

## Page 63: Game

# Topic 7

## Page 65: What does it mean?

Check your answers with the Key Words panel on page 64.

## Page 67: Family Tree

There are many possible sentences.

If you can, check yours with a native speaker.

## Page 68: Family Tree

## Page 68: Questions and answers

형 있어요?

어머니 이름이 뭐예요?

누나 있어요?

형 이름이 뭐예요?

아버지 이름이 뭐예요?

이름이 뭐예요?

어디에서 왔어요?

제 어머니 이름은 사라예요.

아니오, 누나 없어요.

아버지 이름은 팀이에요.

저는 미국 시카고에서 왔어요.

저는 로버트예요.

형 이름은 마크예요.

네, 있어요.

## Page 71: How many?

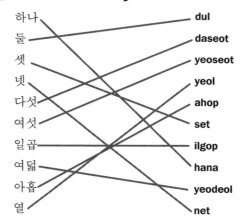

하나 — dul
둘 — daseot
셋 — yeoseot
넷 — yeol
다섯 — ahop
여섯 — set
일곱 — ilgop
여덟 — hana
아홉 — yeodeol
열 — net

## Page 71: Korean sums

1 다섯; 2 여덟; 3 여섯; 4 열둘; 5 둘;
6 열; 7 둘; 8 하나; 9 아홉

## Page 72: My family

There are many possible sentences.

If you can, check yours with a native speaker.

## Topic 8
### Page 75: What does it mean?
Check your answers with the Key Words panel on page 74.

### Page 75: The tools of the trade

### Page 77: Listen and note
1 *First name:* Chanho; *Family name:* Park; *Nationality:* Korean; *Spouse:* Mikjeong Jo; *Children:* 2; *Occupation:* engineer

2 *First name:* Kelly; *Family name:* Brown; *Nationality:* American; *Spouse:* John; *Children:* none; *Occupation:* accountant

### Page 78: What does it mean?
1d, 2e, 3c, 4a, 5b

### Page 78: Which word?
제 __3__ 은 헤리예요. 저는 __6__
입니다. 저는 호주 멜본에서 왔어요.
제 __1__ 이름은 저스틴이에요.
그리고 저는 __4__ 가 세 명이에요.
__2__ 한 명, 딸 __5__ 있어요.

### Page 80: Word Square
factory, school, restaurant, hospital, office, theater, store, bank

| 병 | 명 | 처 | 공 | 장 | 버 | 니 | 학 |
|---|---|---|---|---|---|---|---|
| 원 | 입 | 틴 | 거 | 턴 | 있 | 근 | 교 |
| 은 | 뉴 | 가 | 턴 | 식 | 당 | 캐 | 요 |
| 사 | 무 | 실 | 는 | 다 | 는 | 교 | 멜 |
| 멜 | 입 | 인 | 차 | 주 | 입 | 극 | 인 |
| 택 | 가 | 자 | 주 | 에 | 버 | 장 | 탁 |
| 공 | 계 | 크 | 교 | 리 | 다 | 기 | 자 |
| 주 | 제 | 비 | 교 | 은 | 행 | 제 | 요 |

### Page 81: What are they saying?
1e, 2d, 3a, 4f, 5b, 6c

### Page 82: Which word?
제 이름은 김 병수 __5__ 저는 __2__ 예요. 한국 부산에서
왔어요. 저는 뉴욕에 있는 한국 식당에서 __6__ . 제 __4__
는 선생님이에요. 식당 __8__ 에 있는 아주 큰 __3__ 일 해
요. 저희는 __7__ 이 두 명 있어요. 둘 다 __1__ 학생이에요.

## Test Yourself
### Page 84: May I have...?
1 차 주세요. **cha juseyo;** 2 녹차 주세요. **nokcha juseyo;**
3 케이크 주세요. **keikeu juseyo;** 4 떡볶이 주세요.
**tteokbokki juseyo;** 5 튀김 주세요. **twigim juseyo;**
6 샌드위치 주세요. **saendeuwichi juseyo**

### Page 85: Listen and check
1 True; 2 False; 3 True; 4 False; 5 False; 6 False

### Page 85: Which word?
저는 박 진희예요. __7__ 에 있는 __1__ 도시 인천에서 왔어요.
저는 __8__ 예요. 영국에 있는 작은 한국학교에서 일 해요.
제 __2__ 은 의사예요. 한국학교 옆에 있는 큰 __4__ 에서 일해요.
저희는 __5__ 가 네 명 있어요. 아들 __3__ 그리고 __6__ 이
세 명이에요.

### Page 86: Read and check
1 True; 2 True; 3 False; 4 True; 5 False; 6 True; 7 True; 8 False

### Page 87: Read and check
Check your answers with the Key Words panel on page 64.

### Page 87: How do you say it?
1 제 남편은 의사예요. **je nampyeon-eun uisa-yeyo**
2 저는 여동생이 한 명 있어요. **jeoneun yeodonsaengi han myeong isseoyo**
3 제 아들은 엔지니어예요. **je adeul-eun enjinieoyeyo**
4 진희씨 어머니는 대전에서 왔어요. **jinhi-ssi eomeoni-neun daejeon-eseo wasseoyo**
5 제 아내 이름은 클레어예요. **je anae ireum-eun keulleeo-yeyo**
6 제 오빠는 배우예요. **je oppa-neun baeuyeyo**
7 저는 아이가 없어요. **jeo-nun aiga eopsseoyo**
8 저는 딸이 세 명이에요. **jeoneun ttari se myeong-ieyo**

### Page 88: At the tourist office
안녕히 가세요 **annyeonghi gaseyo** *goodbye (to s.o. leaving)*
안녕히 계세요 **annyeonghi gyeseyo** *goodbye (to s.o. staying)*
안녕하세요 **annyeong haseyo** *hello*
고맙습니다 **gomap-seumnida** *thank you*
뒤 **dwi** *behind*
오른쪽 **oreunjjok** *right*
왼쪽 **oenjjok** *left*
버스 **beoseu** *bus*
근처 **geuncheo** *near*
큰 **keun** *big*
박물관 **bakmulguan** *museum*
어디? **eodi** *where?*

**Name cards:**

| 진희 | 영철 | 민준 | 수진 |
|------|------|------|------|
| 사라 | 메리 | 헨렌 | 리사 |
| 로버트 | 팀 | 켄 | 마크 |

**Sentence-build cards:**

| 이 | 안녕하세요 | 이에요 | 저는 |
|-----|-----------|--------|------|
| 씨 | 뭐예요 | 안녕히 계세요 | |
| ? | 이름 | 안녕히 가세요 | |
| . | 고맙습니다 | 천만에요 | |

| | | | |
|---|---|---|---|
| **Sujin** | **Minjun** | **Yeongcheol** | **Jinhi** |
| **Lisa** | **Helen** | **Mary** | **Sarah** |
| **Mark** | **Ken** | **Tim** | **Robert** |

| | | | |
|---|---|---|---|
| **I** | **am/are/is** | **hello** | *(subject particle* **-i**) |
| **goodbye** *(to someone staying)* | **what is?** | | *(name title* **-ssi**) |
| **goodbye** *(to someone leaving)* | **name** | | **?** |
| **you're welcome** | **thank you** | | **.** |

# GAME CARD ❸ (see page 33)

## Picture cards:

# GAME CARD ❹ (see page 43)

## Cut-out pictures (cut round small pictures)

## Sentence-build cards:

| 안에 | 위에 | 밑에 | 앞에 |
|---|---|---|---|
| 뒤에 | 옆에 | 없어요 | 있어요 |
| 고양이 | 없어요 | 이에요 | 예요 |
| 샌드위치 | 침대 | 탁자 | 소파 |
| 창문 | 의자 | 텔레비전 | 컴퓨터 |
| 전화 | 그림 | 쥐 | 개 |
| 가 | 이 | 는 | 은 |

| in front of | under | on/above | in(side) |
|---|---|---|---|
| there is/are | there isn't/aren't | next to | behind |
| is/are *(ending in vowel)* | is/are *(ending in consonant)* | isn't/aren't | cat |
| sofa | table | bed | sandwich |
| computer | television | chair | window |
| dog | mouse | picture | telephone |
| *subject particle (-eun)* | *subject particle (-neun)* | *subject particle (-i)* | *subject particle (-ga)* |

# GAME CARD ❺ (see page 53)

## Picture cards:

## Adjective cards:

# GAME CARD ⑥ (see page 63)

## Around-town picture cards:

**You are here**

# GAME CARD ❼ (see page 73)

| | | | |
|---|---|---|---|
| 넷 | 여덟 | 셋 | 열 |
| 여섯 | 아홉 | 하나 | 아홉 |
| 일곱 | 둘 | 넷 | 여덟 |
| 하나 | 열 | 넷 | 열 |

| | | | |
|---|---|---|---|
| 둘 | 여섯 | 넷 | 다섯 |
| 여덟 | 아홉 | 열 | 하나 |
| 넷 | 일곱 | 둘 | 다섯 |
| 다섯 | 아홉 | 열 | 아홉 |

| |
|---|
| 1 |
| 2 |
| 3 |
| 4 |
| 5 |
| 6 |
| 7 |
| 8 |
| 9 |
| 10 |

## Work-place picture cards:

## Profession cards:

| 엔지니어 | 교사 | 점원 | 학생 |
| --- | --- | --- | --- |
| 배우 | 요리사 | 의사 | 회사원 |
| 회계사 | 운전사 | | |